*Dating Paul's Life*

57172

# DATING PAUL'S LIFE

## Robert Jewett

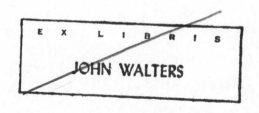
SCM PRESS LTD

Published in the United States and Canada under the title
*A Chronology of Paul's Life*
© Fortress Press 1979

334 00299 0

First British edition published 1979
by SCM Press Ltd
58 Bloomsbury Street, London WC1

Typeset in the United States of America
and printed in Great Britain by
Redwood Burn Limited, Trowbridge & Esher

# CONTENTS

v

# ACKNOWLEDGMENTS

Except for the vicissitudes of scholarly publishing, this book would have appeared in 1966, two years after it was submitted as part of a dissertation at the Eberhard-Karls-University in Tübingen. The study of *Paul's Anthropological Terms*, for which this was originally intended to provide the chronological assumptions, was published out of sequence in 1971. A controversial war and other related projects absorbed a substantial portion of my writing time since the chronology was first ready for publication. Enthusiastic students at Morningside College contributed to keeping my interest alive in the meanwhile. Colleagues in the Paul Seminar and the Pauline Epistles Section of the Society of Biblical Literature provided encouragement. Portions of several summers and other blocks of time were devoted to incorporating new bibliography and clarifying the methodology. The decisive support in this past year, leading to the publication decision by Fortress Press, came from Werner Kelber, Victor Furnish, Gerd Lüdemann, Alfred Suhl, and Walter Schmithals. Their generosity in recommending the publication of a study with which they could not entirely agree is deeply appreciated. And so a project that has occupied a portion of my attention for sixteen years comes to fruition.

My gratitude needs to be expressed to the library staffs in locations where I have pursued this research: the University of Tübingen, the University of Neuchâtel, Yale University, Iliff School of Theology, San Francisco Theological Seminary, the Graduate Theological Union of Berkeley, Claremont School of Theology, North American Baptist Seminary, Luther Seminary, the combined libraries of McCormick Theological Seminary, the Jesuit School of Theology and Lutheran School of Theology at Chicago, Chicago Theological Seminary, and Joseph Regenstein Library at the University of Chicago. The Morningside College library staff has cheerfully processed innumerable requests for interlibrary loans and copies of obscure articles, for which I am especially grateful. I also appreciate the critical aid of colleagues, friends, former students, and professors: John Shelton Lawrence, Richard M. Evans, R. Franklin Terry, John P. Doohen, James T. Clemons, Asher Finkel, Hans Dieter Betz, Walter Taylor, Jr., John C. Hurd, Jr., James Reeder, Raymond Newell, Martin Appelt, Dennis Tevis, Otto Michel, and Otto Betz. Walter and Elizabeth Jewett made suggestions on earlier drafts of the manuscript, and Jan Jewett, my partner in marriage, devoted time to editing and typing. Finally, I owe a debt of gratitude to my editors at Fortress Press, Theodore A. McConnell and Martha Onusconich, for contributing to the final form of the book. By reducing its scope from sixteen to six chapters, we leave the detailed reconstruction of Paul's life and the complicated discussion of the integrity, provenance, and dating of the letters to later studies. Cathlin and Carrol McLaughlin helped in reading proofs while Joan Ayers and Barrie Tritle helped to prepare the indices.

# INTRODUCTION

## THE PROBLEM OF FLUCTUATING EVIDENCE

One of the important unfinished tasks in NT research is to develop a reliable system for dating the Pauline letters. But this is impossible until the major events of his life and ministry are firmly dated to provide a framework upon which to reckon the date of the individual letters. NT scholars have long searched for "absolute dates" from which the rest of the events could be reckoned. The odd thing about this research is that although such dates can fairly well be established, they cannot be fit smoothly into any generally accepted outline of Paul's life. The consequence has been an endless process of date juggling. Studies of the last several decades are no closer to agreement than were those of a generation ago.

The problem of fluctuating dates is perhaps most easily illustrated by glancing at some representative chronologies. Braun and Hahn place the Apostolic Conference in A.D. 43 and Paul's conversion sometime between 27 and 29, agreeing with Haenchen and others that Paul appeared before Festus as a prisoner in the year 55.[1] Suhl generally follows this pattern except that he places the conversion in 30.[2] Buck and Taylor agree on the Festus date but place the conference in 46 and the conversion in 32.[3] Hurd seems to concur with them in placing the collection activities inaugurated by the conference in 46.[4] Lüdemann differs with all of the above in placing the conference in 46, the conversion in 30, and the final Jerusalem trip in 52.[5] Kümmel, Marxsen, Guthrie, Michaelis, Goppelt, and Georgi believe the Apostolic Conference took place in 48 or 49, which would place the conversion sometime in the early thirties.[6] This group of scholars also tends to hold that Paul appeared before Festus and was sent on to Rome in the year 58. Gunther places the conference in 48, moving the conversion back to 31, and sets the appearance before Festus in 59.[7]

1

Ogg agrees on the date of the conference, but places the conversion in 35 and the Festus date in 61.[8] Robinson also agrees on the date of the conference, but places the conversion in 33 and the Festus date in 59.[9] A radically different dating scheme was suggested by Knox who set the conference in 51, the conversion in 37 and the appearance before Festus in 55.[10]

The fluctuation involves almost every aspect of Paul's life. For example, Suggs argued convincingly that the second missionary journey came before instead of after the Apostolic Conference.[11] While Funk made a good case that Luke transposed the "Famine Visit" from its normal position in Acts 24 to its present location in Acts 11, Strecker argued that Luke simply fabricated the account of the "Famine Visit."[12] Even something so basic as the number of Jerusalem journeys fluctuates between the three maintained by Knox, Dockx,[13] and Lüdemann, the four affirmed by Suhl and Ogg, and the five assumed by Robinson, Gunther, and many others. Each of these fluctuations has an important bearing on the dating of the Pauline letters. They cause shifts in the dating of Thessalonians from the second to the third missionary periods; they influence the question of an Ephesian imprisonment and thus the dating of the imprisonment letters; and they require differing answers to the perplexing questions of the date and destination of Galatians. Recent studies by Buck and Taylor, Richards, Hurd, Borse, and Suhl reveal chronic differences of opinion even on the question of the sequence of these letters.[14]

THE NEED FOR A
DEDUCTIVE-EXPERIMENTAL METHOD

In spite of dramatic advances in exegetical method and increasing precision in our knowledge of the factors related to chronology, both the evidence and the conclusions continue to fluctuate as they did a century ago. This is due in part to the persistence of inductive approaches to the material. In his studies of the history of science, Karl R. Popper has described the "Baconian inductivism" that still remains popular in theological and historical research. It aims at cleansing the mind of ". . . prejudices, in order to enable it to recognize the manifest truth . . ."[15] Scholars continue to act as if the pieces of data themselves would somehow compel the truth of Pauline chronology to shine through. Some are convinced that it can only be found by reliance upon evidence from the Book of Acts and others by giving preference to that found in the Pauline letters. The

Baconian inductive method tends to downplay the role of creative intelligence in forming hypotheses, not only regarding the reconciliation of evidence, but even regarding the designation of what constitutes evidence. In contrast, as Carl G. Hempel states, there are ". . . no generally applicable 'rules of induction' by which hypotheses or theories can be mechanically derived or inferred from empirical data . . . Scientific hypotheses and theories are not *derived* from observed facts, but *invented* in order to account for them."[16]

An additional methodological weakness has been the reluctance to subject chronological hypotheses to rigorous tests that might falsify them, or even to develop chronologies. of sufficient specificity that permit their falsification. When so many dates and travel routes are allowed to fluctuate vaguely within broad latitudes, chronologies cannot easily be proven wrong. Such methods achieve no decisive progress in an area where the evidence is internally contradictory, the sources are partially biased, and the theological commitments of scholars remain crucial. The inductivist presuppositions, even when unconsciously followed, are defeated by the fluctuation of each seeming "fact," so.that hypotheses appear to be floating on a sea of variables in which no verification is really possible.

To break this deadlock, I propose that Karl Popper's interpretation of the "unity of scientific method" should be accepted and followed to its conclusion.[17] Every scientific discipline shares the critical approach with history and the humanities, combining appropriate "conjectures" with rigorous "refutations." W. B. Gallie summarizes the viewpoint I would like to adopt, in suggesting that ". . . there is no difference in principle in our general methods of testing as between history and the theoretical sciences."[18] So far as possible, I would like to adapt the deductive-experimental method to the problem of Pauline chronology. I accept Popper's premise that final verifications either of individual pieces of evidence or of scientific hypotheses as a whole are impossible. The best that one can hope for is a demonstration of testability by submitting chronological hypotheses to conditions that could falsify them. This involves establishing a data base of sufficient specificity to make such refutation possible. While there is no way to avoid the role of critical intelligence in defining such data, it is possible to separate this process as far as possible from the creation of hypotheses, and also to respect and utilize the judgments of international scholarship in establishing the margins of probability. Then a chronological hypothesis can be subjected to the crucial test against the data. As Popper shows, such tests can ". . . bring about a decision between two competing theories by refuting (at least) one of them—without, of course, proving the other."[19]

DESIGNING A CHRONOLOGICAL EXPERIMENT

The experimental method is so well-established that it is reflected in the standard logic textbooks of our day. The one most widely used on the American scene, *Introduction to Logic* by Irving M. Copi, suggests the paradigm of a detective, which seems particularly appropriate in relating the experimental method to the complex region of historical investigation.[20] Like the chronologist, the detective seeks to analyze specific, unrepeatable events. He begins with a problem that involves the actions of persons on an irreversible time line. Like the chronologist, he knows that certain things occurred, but must discover precisely when and by whom. Such investigations begin with what Copi calls "preliminary hypotheses." "Everyone, even the most patient and thorough investigator, must pick and choose, deciding which facts to study and which to pass over. One must have some working hypothesis for or against which to collect relevant data."[21] Correspondingly, I begin in Chapter I with the "methodical use of the sources," using the most reliable studies of Acts and the Pauline letters to establish guidelines in the experimental usefulness of evidence. No mere induction suffices here. The exercise of personal critical judgment is essential. Even if my working hypotheses prove false, this step must be taken in order for the experiment to advance our understanding—which means of course that it proves genuinely falsifiable.

The next step for Copi's scientific detective is "collecting additional facts" that can serve ". . . as clues to the final solution."[22] Famous detectives are noted for minute observations of the commonplace, for pursuing the significance of details that seem at first remote. As R. G. Collingwood points out, most historical advances come in similar ways: "The enlargement of historical knowledge comes about mainly through finding how to use as evidence this or that kind of perceived fact which historians have hitherto thought useless to them."[23] I make use of this technique in Chapters II and III, which deal with the ascertainable date–ranges and time–spans in Pauline chronology. Rather than attempting to press the evidence into prematurely precise form, I am content to place *termini a quo et ad quem* on time graphs so that their temporal relationships can be plotted. The interlocking of date–ranges and time–spans with seasonal and other travel data can achieve what any detective gains by constructing scenarios for persons related to a crime. On the assumption that Paul could only have been in one place at a time and hence that a delay in one phase of a time graph causes consequences everywhere along the line, it may be possible to achieve a higher degree of specificity of interpretation for the information that has long been available. The logical coordination of minute details is the historical version of what Popper calls the reduction of "range," the amount of "free play" that a statement of fact allows to reality. When the range is too broad, it becomes impossible to achieve useful testability.[24] The placement of impartially ascertained spans on an irreversible time line allows for such reduction of range and provides a data base that can serve to falsify chronological hypotheses.

Copi observes that collecting additional facts is always closely related to evaluating hypotheses. While a detective may examine a new hypothesis with the discovery of each new fact, the chronologist is able to separate these steps and make positive use of the work of international scholarship. In Chapter IV previous chronological hypotheses are tested against the data base that has been established. Each chronology is viewed as a kind of experiment whose workability is objectively measurable on the basis of the evidence. By avoiding polemics against what Bacon called "the idols of the human mind,"[25] which insert such acrimony into scholarly controversy, the testing of previous hypotheses can be used to discover the underlying causes of the chronological dilemma and to suggest the most promising avenue toward a workable solution. Committed to Popper's admonition that ". . . every refutation should be regarded as a great success,"[26] I assume that failed experiments serve to eliminate options which do not have to be tried again and hence they contribute to the advancement of the quest for truth.

In Chapters V and VI a new hypothesis is developed. The preliminary hypotheses that arose out of the consideration of the sources in Chapter I, and were refined by the examination of previous chronologies in Chapter IV, are crystallized as "the major causes of the chronological dilemma." A new hypothesis is then set forth to eliminate those causes. It is designed to meet Popper's criteria for a successful new theory: "simplicity . . . independently testable" and capable of explaining relationships beyond the hypothesis itself.[27] My hypothesis is that a three–Jerusalem–journeys framework of Paul's life, based on evidence from the Pauline letters, can be correlated with each of the ascertainable date–frames and time–spans when one identifies the second of these journeys for the Apostolic Conference with the trip described in Acts 18:22. Several interlocking time–

spans make it clear that this framework can be correlated with the data base at only one precise location on the time line. But I must insist in advance that the following investigation does not prove the validity of this hypothesis. Consistent with the experimental method, all I wish to claim is that the new hypothesis is not falsified by the crucial test against the evidence. Such tests can falsify theories but are never capable of providing final proof of their validity.[28]

Finally, on the assumption that Copi and others are right and that "a really fruitful hypothesis will explain not only the facts which originally inspired it, but will explain many others in addition,"[29] Chapter VI concludes with a discussion of several important exegetical and historical problems that are potentially solved by the new chronology. To fulfill the requirement that a scientist "must deduce still further consequences from the hypothesis, not for the sake of additional confirmation but for practical use,"[30] the study concludes with a graph of Paul's activities over a 35 year period. Each of the ascertainable date–frames and time–spans is placed on this graph, allowing readers a rapid overview of the interlocking principle. The graph can provide the basis for making precise calculations about travel schedules, missionary campaigns, and communications with churches and colleagues. In lieu of a detailed investigation of the dating of each Pauline epistle, the most likely locations are noted on the graph as an aid to future investigators.

The degree of precision achieved by this new chronology may strike some readers as implying an unwarranted claim of scholarly omniscience. But the experimental perspective remains dominant even in the graph of dates and time–spans. My goal is to provide a chronology of sufficient specificity that it can be falsified by data that already exist or will be discovered by the next generation of scholarly sleuths. Certainty is impossible for mortals to achieve, particularly in an area like NT chronology, but testability is within our grasp. The chapters that follow are designed to offer readers as clear and precise a basis as I can provide to test the conclusions for themselves.

CHAPTER I

# THE METHODICAL USE OF
# THE SOURCES

The main sources for Pauline chronology are Acts and the letters of Paul. Since there are major differences between these two sources, both in the sequence and the structure of Paul's missionary activities, one must begin by understanding the character of each. Such understanding permits one to establish some general principles for the methodical use of evidence in the chronological experiment.

Two problematic tendencies may be discerned in the use of these sources. The first is a concern for harmony that usually seeks to maintain Luke's reputation when conflicts with the letters emerge. The desire to maintain the literal truth or at least the trustworthiness of Scripture and a theological preference for Lukan as compared with Pauline perspective are central to this concern. It results in drawing overly hasty compromises between the sources, occasionally distorting some of the evidence and thus hindering the impartial establishment of ascertainable dates and time-spans.[1]

The second problematic tendency lies in the opposite direction: an undifferentiated skepticism regarding the usability of the Book of Acts in historical reconstructions. Arising out of the discovery of editorial biases, factual mistakes, and some imaginative fabrications by the author of Acts, this skepticism can take the form of outright rejection of all historical data contained in the book or the sporadic rejection of data on the grounds of subjective criteria. The result is an inability and even a lack of interest in distinguishing between the dependable and the spurious. Obsessive skepticism will find reasons to reject every fragment of evidence, whereas it takes a carefully differentiated caution to distinguish between biased details and those suitable for inclusion in a chronological experiment. The elements in such a method must derive from the analysis of the materials

7

themselves. The issue is most pronounced in Acts, which is the appropriate place to begin.

## THE AUTHOR OF LUKE-ACTS AS
## THEOLOGIAN AND HISTORIAN

Since the historical and theological perspective of the author of Luke–Acts has been examined intensively by recent studies,[2] the task here is simply to sketch some guidelines relevant to chronology. After Dibelius demonstrated the radical extent of Luke's editorial work,[3] critical scholars have tended to view him less as a neutral reporter than as a theologian in his own right.[4] Luke can no longer be approached, as did many earlier scholars,[5] on the assumption that he simply related various traditions of the early church. This does not mean that he used no sources and traditions in his book,[6] but it does imply that critical scholarship must take Luke's own theology into consideration at every step in evaluating chronological data.[7]

The author of Acts was at once historian and theologian.[8] What held these roles together was less the Hellenistic traditions of historiography[9] than the author's understanding of salvation–history. In contrast to the two–aeon thinking of Paul, Luke viewed history as a continuing development through the epoch of Israel and the epoch of Jesus to the present—the period of the church. Although he retained a fragment of the early apocalyptic tradition of the day of judgment, he shared neither the intense expectation nor the pessimism about this present age. In fact he viewed his present as an age in which the church possessed the Spirit and was triumphantly engaging in a world mission to the gentiles. To bear witness to this glorious fulfillment, Acts was written. This reveals that Luke stood within the tradition of Jewish historiography, whose aim was to witness to God's action in history.[10] But it also indicates the author's approach to the issues arising in his own time. The problem of the postponed parousia was answered by the proclamation of present fulfillment; the problem of continuity with Israel raised by the inclusion of the uncircumcised was dealt with by the line of divinely ordained history leading from the patriarch's promise to the fulfillment in the church; suspicions that Christianity was politically subversive were thwarted by the claim to be the rightful inheritors of Judaism's legal rights within the empire. Everything depended upon the church's really expressing the divine plan in history.

The author of Luke–Acts thus had theological motivations for idealizing the early church. But rather than making the church of his day appear to conform with the early church, he set forth two connected though distinct periods within the final epoch of the church.[11] The first was that of the early church, characterized by continued devotion to Judaism's law and temple but also by the growing realization under divine pressure that the gentiles must be included. The second period was that of the gentile church, characterized by Paul's missionary work in the West and by the gentiles' acceptance of a modified form of the law in the Apostolic Decree. The decisive link between the former period and that of the author was provided by the Apostolic Conference at which this decree was reportedly enacted and where the gentile mission received the official blessing of the Jerusalem leaders.[12] To ensure continuity with Israel, both periods had their beginnings in Jerusalem. The book reaches its climax when Paul traveled from the holy city to Rome.[13] Since the Jerusalem church was thought of as "the trustee of the Holy Spirit,"[14] the validity of the gentile mission and of Paul's missionary work depended upon Jerusalem's authorization.

Some implications of this theological perspective for the question of Pauline chronology may now be drawn. 1) The author of Luke–Acts has a theological reason for presenting a Jerusalem–centered picture of the activities of Paul. Since this kind of perspective is absent from the Pauline letters themselves, one must carefully examine whether the missionary expeditions really began in Jerusalem and whether Paul was actually dependent upon the Jerusalem authorities. 2) The author has a theological reason to idealize the two periods of the church's history as manifest products of the Spirit. 3) The author also has a theological reason to emphasize the harmony between the mother church at Jerusalem and the gentile churches. Given the conflict–laden picture of early church life that emerges from the Pauline letters, one is forced to examine whether journeys to settle church disputes, imprisonments in ambiguous circumstances, and adverse reactions by public officials were repressed in Acts. 4) Since the periodizing of the church's epochs was shaped by theological considerations, one must cautiously examine the resultant outline of Paul's life and mission. Was the Apostolic Conference really the transitional event that led to an independent Pauline mission and was the Apostolic Decree the product of this conference? 5) Since critical doubt about the chronology of Acts is concentrated at those points where the author's theological perspective gains its clearest expression, it follows that we must give priority to details conflicting with this perspective or not directly serving it. For example, travel and historical details incidentally men-

tioned in the text have a higher claim to accuracy than the overall framework in which they appear. They warrant inclusion in an experiment
whose goal is to test their validity by the test of chronological congruence.

## THE USE OF ORAL AND WRITTEN
## MATERIALS IN ACTS

Form and redaction criticism have cast doubts on the traditional assumption that Luke employed written sources from early church archives for
the bulk of his history. In some instances the traditions appear to have
been oral rather than written and at times the editorial work of the author
is so extensive that it is difficult to reconstruct the original source.[15] This
is especially true with many of the longer episodes that Luke builds so
skillfully.[16] In other sections, however, one finds a non–Lukan style and
theological perspective which indicate the presence of materials whose
distinctiveness is hard to explain without written sources. The insights of
source criticism must therefore be combined with redaction criticism and
form criticism to deal with this evidence.[17]

One indication of written sources is Luke's distinctive habit of writing
editorial summaries to join various sections of his narrative together. The
blocks of materials are relatively self–contained units that sometimes differ
in vocabulary and theology from the editorial summaries joining them
together.[18] Another indication of written materials is the observation made
by Jeremias and others that the account beginning with Acts 6:1 is broken
at 8:4 by an insertion of alien materials (8:5–40). The account is picked up
in 9:1–30, only to be broken again by 9:31–11:18; then in 11:19–30 it
resumes once more.[19] On the basis of literary analysis and a study of the
tendencies of the various strands, the account beginning with 6:1 has
been termed the "Antiochene Source,"[20] comprising roughly the sections
6:1–8:4; 9:1–30; 11:19–30; 12:25–14:23; 15:35ff. Although some have held
that this source continues to the end of Acts, it seems quite unlikely.

The second half of Acts is not nearly so rich in clues indicating the
redaction of written materials. The so-called "we–sections" from 16:11ff.
cannot be separated from the rest of the text on the basis of style or
vocabulary.[21] Although one may argue that the use of the first person
plural is a stylistic device implying the presence of the author at the
scene,[22] or merely the use of an eyewitness report provided by someone
else,[23] it is clear that the author achieved a unity here that contrasts with
the first half of Acts. Here is a careful summary of the matter: "The
second part of Acts is written in a style which is obviously different from

that of the first, though the difference is not susceptible of statistical demonstration and does not exclude a remarkable unity in all parts of the book."[24] It is appropriate, therefore, to recognize that the material related to the first journey (Acts 13–14) differs from that of the later journeys, especially after Acts 16:10. Since the travel reports are the most crucial material for chronology, it is logical to begin the more detailed analysis with Acts 13–14.

The account of the first journey (Acts 13–14) is a continuous narrative, unmarred by editorial transitions or summaries that would suggest an order contrived or readjusted by a redactor. Acts 13:52 could be classed as an insertion or summary similar to 4:32ff. or 9:31,[25] but it clearly does not serve as an artificial transition between two sections. Paul and Barnabas are already in Iconium in 13:51 and likewise in 14:1. Yet the narrative is void of precise travel details which later accounts such as 16:11ff. or 20:6ff. provide. Nor are there references to persons other than the apostles whose existence can be historically verified. It was partly on account of these contrasts with the later travel reports that Johannes Weiss concluded that Luke had recast much of this material.[26] More recently, Ernst Haenchen has argued that this section was a Lukan composition,[27] noting, however, that it was completely different in style from the accounts of the second and third missionary expeditions.[28] It seems paradoxical to declare Acts 13–14 to be Lukan in composition despite these stylistic differences from generally recognized Lukan materials, but at any event Haenchen does succeed in demonstrating that Acts 13–14 was not based on an eyewitness itinerary.

One may logically infer that these two chapters were not originally composed by the author of the rest of Acts. This is suggested not only by the differences in style and vocabulary, but also by the peculiar point of view in this section. Luke's interest was to show the missionary work of Paul as centering in Jerusalem. Yet Acts 13–14 pictures the first epoch-making expedition as originating at and returning to Antioch rather than Jerusalem.[29] If Acts 15:1–34 is an insertion by the redactor, as many commentators assume, the narrative of 14:28 would have originally continued in 15:35ff., thus stating explicitly that Paul and Barnabas did not visit Jerusalem or anywhere else upon returning from the first missionary journey. The best explanation of these details seems to be that Acts 13–14 was part of the pre–Lukan material originating in Antioch,[30] designed to emphasize the independent role of the Antioch congregation. An objection to this view is that a congregation believing in an imminent parousia would have no reason to commit memoirs to writing for the sake of the coming generations.[31] That such a congregation would not compose this kind of document for posterity is clear, but there is no reason why it would not do so for polemic reasons in its own day.[32] The polemic is clearly aimed against Jerusalem, as indicated by the lack of any reference to Peter,[33] by the commencement of the account with the report of unfairness on the part of Jerusalem leaders to the Hellenistic widows (Acts 6:1ff.), and by the emphasis on the successful western mission as resulting from the obedience to the Spirit by the Antioch leaders. The best surmise is that the material in Acts 13–14 was formed from the Antioch recollection of the reports rendered by Barnabas and Paul at the conclusion of the journey. This would explain the episodic character of these chapters as well as the lack of precise travel details. Though there is no reason to doubt the essential correctness of the sequence of towns visited, the details are so vague that the journey cannot be precisely dated.

This analysis sheds some preliminary light on the possible use of Acts in a chronological hypothesis. The author apparently does not conjure the missionary journeys out of his own imagination. He uses written materials to some extent, and he does not revise them to the degree that their original character is completely obscured.[34] Despite the fact that the Antiochene Source did not agree with all of the author's inclinations, he simply placed it in his pro–Jerusalem framework and added editorial transitions to smooth over the gaps. The style, vocabulary, and theological intention of his transitions are discernibly different from those of his sources. This makes an uncompromisingly skeptical use of Acts unnecessary, for if one can differentiate between materials that the writer used and the added editorial transitions, then the points at which he has manipulated the evidence can be readily discovered. If, as Haenchen puts it, Luke ". . . joins short, compact, picturesque scenes together like the stones of a mosaic,"[35] the connecting pattern will be more suspect historically than the stones themselves.

The travel accounts in Acts 15:36ff. are more important than earlier sections for the immediate task, entering the realm of verifiable history with the references to Gallio (18:12), Felix (23:24ff.), and Festus (24: 27ff.). The frequent allusions to travel plans and to the presence or movements of Paul's co–workers in the letters may be correlated with information in this section of Acts. Imbedded in this second half of Acts are precise travel details that initially appear to have been made by a person traveling with Paul. Although these sections cannot be separated stylistically from the remaining narrative, they may be distinguished by the peculiar nature of the details they provide. Whereas 15:56–16:10 tells only in general terms what Paul did and where he went, suddenly in 16:11ff. it is reported not only that he "sailed" but also how long the journey lasted. The same detailed accounting is evident in many places through to the end of Acts (cf. 16:12–13; 17:1–9, 10, 14–15; 20:4–21:26; 27:1–28:16). These sections may be easily distinguished from other travel references that are summarized in a manner reminiscent of the summaries in the first half of Acts (cf. 16:6–8; 18:1; 19:1; 20:1–3). A decisive observation is that the so–called "we-sections" are in every case those that present details of the precise quality now under discussion. The person who reports these travels has quite a different interest and power of observation from the person or group who wrote the account for the first missionary expedition in Acts 13–14. He who provided the detailed travel references in the second half of Acts had an interest in things for their own sake, an interest which must be called "historical" when compared with the standards of classical historiography.[36] Since these precise details are provided for only a portion of Paul's travels and since they are never used in the explicit service of Luke's periodization as such, they appear useful to the historian.[37]

The debate over the use and/or origin of the "we-source" has not arrived at a satisfactory consensus. However, as Erich Grässer observes in his recent account of the controversy, there is solid agreement on the shape of the dilemma. The abrupt appearance of the "we" materials seems to favor a theory that Luke incorporated sporadic eyewitness accounts originally created by others, while the stylistic unity between the "we-sections" and the rest of the second half of Acts speaks for the theory of Lukan provenance.[38] Conservative scholars have tended to favor the idea that Luke made use of his own travel diary in the "we-sections," while Grässer, Conzelmann, Haenchen, and others are convinced that the theological and historical discrepancies between Acts and the letters eliminates the possibility of authorship by a companion. Neither side is very convincing.[39] The argument for Lukan authorship appears motivated by the concern to provide *a priori* grounds for accepting the authenticity of the travel details. This violates the experimental methodology I would favor in settling issues such as this; it also leads defenders to minimize the discrepancies between Acts and the Pauline letters. On the other hand, the denial of Lukan authorship in the "we-sections" presupposes that modern scholars know the limits beyond which ancient writers could not or would not go in altering details to create desired impressions. Despite the certainty with which such opinions are advanced, no historical law can be adduced on this point.

Several major theories have been advanced to explain the dilemma concerning the "we-source." Ernst Haenchen suggests that Luke used the first person plural as a stylistic device to denote the presence of eye-witness materials at certain points.[40] This overlooks the fact that some of his other materials from oral tradition also stemmed from eyewit-nesses. Why would a writer invite the suspicion that some of his infor-mation was of inferior quality by inserting "we" in some places and not in others? Moreover, as Vielhauer concludes from the analysis of classical historiography, the use of the first person does not provide emphasis of the kind Haenchen has in mind.[41] Neither the stylistic unity of the second half of Acts nor the sporadic use of "we" is accounted for by this theory. Eckhard Plümacher answers some of these objections by pointing to the stress in classical historiography on gaining experience in travel as a way to become a genuine historian. Since the "we-passages" are al-ways related to sea travel, the insertion of the first person plural indicates the author of Luke-Acts is an experienced sailor.[42] Plümacher acknowl-edges that there is no parallel in classical history for such a use of the first person form, but if the details are actually fictitious, this is a better explanation than Haenchen's. Their fictive character is not so much proven as assumed. Plümacher follows the critical view of the past seventy-five years in assuming "the substantial ignorance of Luke about the life of Paul"[43]—another way of saying that Acts presents a highly tinted portrait. If deliberate falsifications are proven, then the entire issue would obviously require rethinking. A further weakness in Plü-macher's hypothesis is that the sailing details in Acts 13–14 and 18:18–20 are not advertised by the first person plural. Are we to assume that the redactor forgot to flaunt his decisive seagoing experience in recounting those episodes? Clearly Plümacher's theory cannot fully explain the strangely sporadic quality of the "we-source."

As Grässer observes, the most serious discussion of the "we-source" in recent years has revolved around the itinerary hypothesis of Martin Dibelius.[44] He set aside the question of authorship in order to gain a more objective picture on stylistic grounds, concluding that ". . . an itinerary . . . with notes of his journeys, of the founding of communities and of the result of evangelizing" provided the "framework for the cen-tral part of Acts."[45] Several important observations sustain Dibelius' view.

1) The uniformity of the treatment of travel stations reveals that the information did not derive from gathering local traditions. 2) The inclusions of theologically insignificant details, "which serve neither to edify nor to entertain,"[46] reveal the use of travel notes. 3) The style and language of the "we–passages are not essentially different from other passages which deal with similar events."[47] Dibelius follows these observations part way to their logical conclusion in arguing that the author of Luke–Acts ". . . introduced his 'we' into an account which he had, in order to indicate when he was present."[48] He avoids the traditional "eyewitness" theory because of the highly literary quality of the sea adventure in Acts 27, but assumes that the author was present there also. The conclusion should be obvious, but subsequent debate avoided it. A. D. Nock hypothesized the presence of a series of travel diaries utilized by the author of Luke–Acts.[49] His description of classical analogues was taken up by Philipp Vielhauer and hotly disputed by Gottfried Schille and Eckhard Plümacher.[50] Vielhauer is congratulated by Grässer[51] for having made the quantum leap toward a solution by separating the itinerary from the author of Luke–Acts—but this succeeds only in confusing the facts concerning the stylistic unity of the second half of Acts.

The simplest explanation for the sporadic appearance of the "we–sections" and their stylistic similarity with the rest of Acts is that the author used his own travel notes, giving them distinctive personal embellishments. Critical scholars would prefer to avoid this explanation because it so easily leads to a facile assumption that the details in the diary have an *a priori* legitimacy. I share the concern about naively accepting such details as historical and prefer to speak of "experimental usability," so that the question of historicity can be tested in an objective, experimental procedure. I also share the critical view that there are substantial differences between the picture of Paul in Acts as compared with the letters, but hesitate to follow the logic of those differences toward a conclusion that violates the widely observed facts concerning the "we–sections."

There is at least one segment of the first person plural narrative proving conclusively that the author of Luke–Acts kept the initial diary, was involved in the travels, and consciously altered details to suit his redactional goals. A consideration of Acts 20:13–17 as a kind of test case for the "we-sections" lays the basis for a logical solution. The internal contradictions in this passage have been visible to exegetes for at least a generation, but their relevance for the question of the "we–sections" has not been noted. For some reason the redactor feels impelled to explain why the ship selected for the trip to Jerusalem went from Chios to Samos and thence to Miletus, avoiding Ephesus. That Paul made this decision "so that he might not have to spend time in Asia; for he was hastening to be in Jerusalem, if possible, on the day of Pentecost," (Acts 20:16) is refuted in the following verse. Paul broke the journey in Miletus and sent a messenger back to Ephesus to gather the elders for a farewell address, which would have required a round trip back to the port they had just passed over to save time. As Conzelmann and Haenchen point out, this would have caused a delay of three to five days. In all probability Paul avoided Ephesus because of the troubles he had experienced with the Roman authorities there.[52]

The redactional modification is consistent with Luke's purposes in picturing Paul's amiable relations with the Roman government, and implying that he was a piously observant Jew. But the key question is one any shrewd detective would ask: Why does the author of Acts provide this fallacious excuse in the first place? He does not seem overly concerned about the dozens of other important cities that Paul and his colleagues pass by in their other travels. Obviously he knows something about the Ephesian situation and the related travel arrangements that he wishes to conceal. Since he understands that such knowledge would contradict the picture he wishes to create, he alters details that readers far from the scene would never have reflected on. Moreover, it is clear that the "we-source" is more than a redactional invention. Why invent something you have to refute? Why create an illogical explanation if you feel free to change an itinerary you had merely invented to show how experienced a sailor you are?

Acts 20:13-17 is most easily explained as a written itinerary that has obscure, negative implications from the redactor's point of view, and this implies that he was either very close to or identical with the person who wrote the "we-source." Only someone with direct knowledge of the travel decisions in the 50s could know enough to worry about these details. Furthermore, this section reveals that Luke has no compunction about adjusting details for theological and literary reasons. This provides a crucial argument against the current dogma that Luke could not have been Paul's companion because of factual discrepancies between Acts and the letters. In this instance, proximity rather than distance between the redactor and the historical events is revealed by the discrepancy. When one correlates this crucial section of the "we-source" with the stylistic unity in the second half of Acts, it becomes clear that the person providing the detailed travel account is the redactor of Luke–Acts—whether that person was Luke, as tradition has held, or someone else.[53] Leaving aside the complicated and largely unanswerable questions about the authorship and precise dating of Luke–Acts,[54] I can only conclude that the evidence within the text itself compels the belief that the author of Acts made use of travel notes that he himself had written and that the "we" was simply retained from the notes themselves.

It is important to insist, however, that this conclusion does not imply that any of the details in the so–called "we–source" have an intrinsic credibility. As the next section will argue, there are additional places where the redactor appears to consciously alter details to fit his purposes. Only within the context of a deductive method, which eliminates details that clearly have been manipulated, and then experiments with those that are left, is one in a position to assess the credibility of what remains. Pious claims of Lukan authorship can throw no more light on the issue than an inventive skepticism that presumes to know more about who could not have written Acts than about who did.

One of the most significant features of the traditions utilized in Acts is what Olof Linton called the "third–aspect." He noted that Paul's Judaizing opponents in Galatia circulated some of the false reports of Paul's life which later found their way into Luke's account.[55] Just as the Galatian troublemakers said that Paul had traveled to Jerusalem soon after conversion and remained with the apostles for a long time to learn about the gospel (Gal. 1:15–20), so Acts tells its readers that Paul spent considerable time with the apostles in Jerusalem soon after his conversion (Acts 9:26–30).[56] The remarkable thing was that the Paulinists and the Judaizers both had an interest in stressing Paul's close ties with the Jerusalem church; the former would stress that the original apostles had agreed with Paul's gospel to the gentiles, while the latter wished to show that Paul was subordinate to the Jerusalem church. The concern to organize Paul's life as a long series of Jerusalem journeys did not originate with Luke, even though it was consistent with his theology. He appears to have used materials that Paul's enemies first created, accepting such information and rumors in favor of what he may well have known to be historically correct because he preferred to be theologically correct.[57]

## THE EVIDENCE OF REDACTIONAL DISTORTIONS

Having noted the use of traditional materials in Acts, it is now appropriate to direct attention to locations where the author's editorial work is particularly manipulative.[58] If a general pattern of altering traditional materials can be discerned, further guidelines can be established for using chronological evidence.

Acts 18:18ff., a passage crucial to the establishment of a chronology, bears clear signs of editorial insertions and corrections. This account of Paul's journey from Corinth to Jerusalem at the end of the so-called second missionary journey is strangely disjointed and compressed. V. 18d is appended so loosely to the sentence that it has long been debatable whether it was Paul or Aquila who shaved his head. Since no precedent has been found for head shaving as a Jewish rite performed outside of Jerusalem, where Nazarite vows had to be performed,[59] this serves to arouse one's suspicions that Luke inserted his afterthoughts to answer the question of Paul's motivation in undertaking the dangerous trip to Jerusalem.[60] A second insertion of vv. 19b–21a must likewise be ascribed to Luke's correction of his materials. If this insertion were deleted there would be a normal connection between vv. 19a and 21b. Haenchen has suggested that Luke's motivation in making this insertion was to allay any thought that Paul did not in fact establish the Ephesian church. So Paul is pictured as preaching the first sermon and laying the foundation for a Jewish Christian church which did not separate itself from the synagogue until his return to Ephesus.[61] Disregarding the additions for the moment, one notes an extremely brief account of the departure for Syria,[62] the stopover in Ephesus where Aquila and Priscilla disembarked, and the arrival in Caesarea followed by the greeting of the Jerusalem church. This compressed account of a Jerusalem trip is set in a section where Luke's information seems to be entirely secondhand. The last precise travel detail came in Acts 17:15. In 20:4 one begins to find such details again. The repeated correction of his materials and the lack of precise details all arouse our caution. Here Luke reveals that either he is not in possession of adequate information or that he wished to alter the impressions that his sources would otherwise have made.

The report of the Ephesian ministry appears equally suspicious (Acts 18:24ff.). Here again Luke makes obvious attempts to give his readers a well-manicured impression. The flattering portrayal of Apollos' activities in 18:24, 25a, b, 26a, 27 and 28 is broken up by censurious editorial comments (18:25c, 26b) on grounds that Apollos did not teach Christian baptism and had to be instructed by Paul's workers, Priscilla and Aquila.[63] Probably Luke makes use here of an Ephesian tradition that was favorable to Apollos.[64] The presence of material with a bias different from Luke's indicates that his own notes are not being corrected here. Further evidence of editorial work may be seen in the phrase *hōs de splērōthē tauta* (Acts 19:21a), which connects best with the narrative of the activities in Ephesus (19:8–10), the report of Paul's powerful exorcisms and the burning of the magic books having been inserted at this point. As one analyzes this material in detail it becomes clear that the weaving of episodes solves some serious theological dilemmas for the redactor. The account of Paul's plans to leave Ephesus (19:21–22) is pointedly included before the story of the riot, with the apparent intention of spiking any suspicion that Paul was driven out of town by the disturbance.[65] Considering the improbability of the account of the silversmith riot—in which Luke pictured Paul as being covertly protected by the rulers (Acts 19:31, 35–41)—one must seriously consider the possibility that this was the shattering event that Paul reported in Ephesus (1 Cor. 15:32). In all probability an Ephesian imprisonment provided the conclusion of his ministry there. In short, although there is no reason to doubt the information in 19:8–10 concerning the length of Paul's stay in Ephesus,[66] a welter of conflicting and sharply edited details arouse suspicion that Luke was seeking to touch up the picture of what actually happened.

The report of the last Jerusalem journey likewise contains indications that the author was striving to create a picture that his evidence could not support. Luke fails to provide an adequate motivation for this journey taken in face of mortal danger. As the Pauline letters reveal, the true purpose of this journey was to deliver the offering to the Jerusalem church.[67] But Luke excises all but one incidental reference to the offering, possibly meaning to imply that Paul felt he must return to the mother church to confer about the Roman expedition before he dared embark upon it (cf. Acts 19:21). Luke suggests no purpose for the rendezvous with representatives from the church at Troas (20:4), who had in all probability brought the offerings from their congregations to be sent on to Jerusalem. But Luke's deliberate veiling[68] of the true purpose for this fateful journey left the unexplained circumstances there for one to read. Furthermore the redactor did not succeed in erasing the last reference to the offering, for in Acts 24:17 Paul is pictured as explaining his presence in Jerusalem by reference to the offering he wished to deliver to his "nation."[69] This is not the only example of redactional discrepancy. It has often been observed that Paul was notified of the Apostolic Decree in Acts 21:25, as if he had never heard of it before; yet this was exactly the decree he was supposed to have accepted in Acts 15:29.[70]

Volker Stolle's study of the redaction of Acts 21–26 helps place these observations within the larger context of Luke's picture of Paul.[71] He suggests that the following passages were redactional insertions into an already coherent account of Paul's hearings and trial: Acts 21:18-26; 21:37-22:22; 22:30-23:10; 24:20b-21; 24:24-26; 25:9-11; 25:13-26:32. When these passages are set aside, a historically reliable account of Paul's arrest, imprisonment, and trials emerges that retains the chronologically significant connection with Felix and Festus as well as the key legal details that have impressed Roman historians such as Sherwin-White.[72] Stolle does not speculate on the authorship of the original account, but similarities in vocabulary and style between the original and the material inserted by the redactor as well as the relative coherence of the final version make it plausible in my view that the author of the "we-source" original was the final editor. In this instance, a more reliable original account, probably written close to the time of the events themselves, was edited to downplay Paul's effort to seal the connection between the gentile and the Jerusalem churches and to travel past Rome to Spain. Luke, or whoever the redactor was, transformed the events into a divinely planned campaign to proclaim the gospel to Jewish and Roman officialdom.[73] Paul the apostle is transformed into a witness to the claims of the risen Jesus, a catalyst of the conflict initiated by Jesus himself that is so visible in Jesus' trial and execution.[74]

The discovery of such discrepancies between original sources and Luke's redactional work allows one to concentrate historical attention on details whose experimental usability is enhanced by their escape from the heavy hand of theologically motivated alterations. Far from reducing the usability of Acts, the presence of such revealing clues gives confidence. They show that Luke was by no means a genius who rearranged every geographical and historical detail with cunning precision.[75] Rather he was one who left telltale marks on and between the sources he used, thus offering the historian a basis to distinguish between spurious and experimentally useful chronological details.

## THE EXPERIMENTAL VALUE OF
## DETAILS IN ACTS

It is now appropriate to draw conclusions about the usefulness of chronological information in the Book of Acts. At a number of points the theological motivation of the redactor has manifested itself in areas relevant to chronology.[76] The framework of five Jerusalem journeys, the downplaying of embarrassing conflicts in the churches and with the civil authorities, and the motivation for the final Jerusalem journey all fall under suspicion. Whenever a chronological detail stands under the impact of such redactional manipulation, it loses its potential for inclusion in a chronological hypothesis. On the other hand, whenever the original sources of Acts surface, the details appear to be more useful. There is of course no *a priori* basis to affirm the absolute validity of any such details, but they nevertheless seem suited for the chronological experiment proposed here. References to public figures such as Claudius (Acts 11:28; 18:2), Agrippa (12:1), Sergius Paulus (13:7), Gallio (18:12), Felix (23:6), Festus (24:27), Ananias (23:2) and others seem largely usable because there is no attempt to correlate them with the Lukan chronological framework.[77] The exception is Acts 11:27ff., where Luke attempts to date the famine collection "in the days of Claudius" and states that Agrippa's persecution began "about that time." When Luke fits the details in this way into his chronological scheme one must be very skeptical. But when he does not attempt to fit a date into his salvation–history framework, a more positive evaluation is warranted. In fact, of the 57 instances where Acts provides an exact statement of days, months, or years, there are no other examples of explicit chronological manipulation. The redactor neither adds up cumulative totals nor connects the details with an overall chronological scheme. Except for the instance noted above, the author does not peg such details to specific years on the Roman or the Jewish calendar, as, for example, Josephus so often does.

The experimental usability of these details is augmented further by their accurate correlation with administrative and judicial arrangements in the Mediterranean world of the mid–first century. A. N. Sherwin–White's extensive investigation of legal and social details confirmed their dependability while demonstrating how difficult it would have been for a second century redactor to piece together an accurate account from Roman archives. The conclusion of this secular historian goes somewhat further than an experimental perspective would require. "For Acts the confirmation of historicity is overwhelming. Yet Acts is, in simple terms and judged externally, no less of a propaganda narrative than the Gospels, liable to similar distortions. But any attempt to reject its basic historicity even in matters of detail must now appear absurd."[78] Sherwin–White has been cited by Ward Gasque to support a sweepingly affirmative view of Acts' credibility, overlooking the theological distortions to which the Roman historian alludes. Gasque even deletes the "propaganda" proviso from his citation of this paragraph.[79] While remaining skeptical of the form–critical method, Sherwin–White's study is not an apologetic defense of Luke.

Luke's penchant for precision results in a considerable body of information usable in a chronological experiment. He differentiates between a "full year" (11:26) and "three months" (20:3); he does not simply round off a year and a part of a second year into "two years" as was customary at times in the ancient world, but he specifies "a year and six months" (18:11) or "two years" (24:27). This precision, when presented without theological motivation and when found in a document in which the majority of the events remain undated, calls forth a cautious credence. In those 36 instances where Luke gives a general designation of time, such as "after some days" or "after many days," Harnack concluded that in all but a few instances these designations reflected a fairly substantial grasp of how long things actually lasted.[80] They do not appear to be used carelessly to disguise the author's ignorance. The many instances in which no temporal designation is provided indicate that the author is not afraid of silence when he has no information.

This affirmation of the experimental usefulness of the incidental chronological details should not be extended to Luke's references to Jewish festivals.[81] Since Luke erroneously depicts Paul as continuing in an orthodox obedience to Jewish laws, the references to Paul's eagerness to commemorate the Jewish festivals (e.g., 20:16; 27:9) should be read with skepticism.[82] The fact that Paul himself reckoned seasons on the basis of the Jewish festivals (1 Cor. 16:8) and behaved "as one under the law" (1 Cor. 9:20) in his missionary strategy should not be taken to mean he celebrated the Jewish festivals with legalistic devotion.

## THE SUPERIOR VALUE OF DETAILS FROM THE PAULINE LETTERS

The Pauline letters contain a considerable body of data that can be used in chronological research. The numerous references to events and activities in his previous life[83] may be correlated with the references to his previous travels.[84] In addition there are many references to Paul's travel plans[85] and to the movements and activities of his co–workers.[86] One of these references is to a person whose life can be dated by extra-biblical means: in 2 Cor. 11:32–33 Paul speaks of the ethnarch of King Aretas.[87] It is important to note, however, that the motive for mentioning Aretas is not chronological. Paul is relating at this point the scandalous events of his previous life which reveal how God provides him with strength in weakness.[88] The same could be said about Gal. 1:13–2:14 where Paul's most extensive description of his former life is found. Here he defends his independence against the slanders of the Judaizers who maintained among other things that he had made many obedient trips to the Jerusalem authorities.[89] Paul specifically denies having made more than two such trips prior to the writing of Galatians. Since the first visit lasted a mere fifteen days, three years after his conversion (Gal. 1:18), this sustains his claim of independence. In fact, he points out, he went far away to Arabia immediately after his conversion (Gal. 1:17). Since it was fourteen years before he returned to Jerusalem (Gal. 2:1) for the Apostolic Conference, one could scarcely term him an emissary of the Jerusalem authorities. He was so loosely connected to Jerusalem that the Judean church could not even recognize his face (Gal. 1:22). All this makes it plain that Paul's goal in Galatians is not to establish a chronology as such but rather to document the independence of his apostleship.[90] He makes no effort to date his Jerusalem visits according to current calendars, only being interested in the time–spans between them. Since Paul accompanies his claims with the most solemn asseveration of accuracy before God (Gal. 1:20), one hesitates to doubt his word.[91]

These data from the letters have intrinsic superiority over anything contained in Acts. In the first place they are the earliest information available to us, antedating the material in Acts by a number of years, if not decades. Second, these details are not motivated by chronological considerations or any assumption regarding the periodization of the church's history. Third, material from letters such as these must be classed as primary historical data and thus have an intrinsic priority over secondary materials such as a history of the type Luke works out. This evaluation does not depend upon theological or personal criteria; whether one is theologically inclined toward Paul or Luke, the fact remains that methodical considerations force one to give unequivocal priority to chronological details in the letters.

The result is that the general outline of Paul's life must be worked out on the basis of the evidence from the letters and these alone. This means one must break with Luke's framework of five different trips to Jerusalem after Paul's conversion, and one must seriously investigate the possibility of articulating Pauline chronology on the basis of the three Jerusalem journeys and the various phases of missionary activity reflected in the letters. To compromise between Luke's general outline and that reflected in the Pauline letters is to open the door to a subjective chaos that can never be tamed by the whim of the scholar. A general rule therefore is that material from Acts is usable in the chronological experiment only when it does not conflict with evidence in the letters.

# CHAPTER II

# THE EXTERNALLY ASCERTAINABLE DATE–RANGES

Having established guidelines in the use of evidence, the first step in the chronological experiment is to ascertain the dates of events and persons mentioned in Acts and the letters. This chapter analyzes those that can be correlated with external evidence from secular history and archeology. To make the experiment as impartial as possible, it is essential to establish each date independently. The bearing of each date on the others must never be allowed to intrude in the analysis. Since many of the dates can be established only within margins of probability, a graph system will be employed, setting the *termini a quo* and *ad quem*. A more precise assignment of dates within these margins will await construction of the chronological hypothesis.

Unfortunately there is no useful chronological evidence from the period prior to Paul's conversion. The effort to date his birth on the basis of his possible rabbinic ordination around the age of forty, prior to his participation in the persecution of early Christians,[1] fails because of the lack of clear evidence that he carried therein a truly judicial function.[2] Such a reckoning at any event would depend upon the dating of the persecution, which is itself dependent on an uncertain reckoning between the dates of the crucifixion and Paul's conversion.[3] That Paul was a native of Tarsus[4] does not have direct chronological relevance, unless one were to accept the highly improbable reference by Jerome to a rumor that the apostle's parents emigrated there from Gischala shortly after the death of Herod the Great.[5] The reference in Acts 22:3 to Paul's study with Gamaliel, hotly disputed as it is,[6] would allow a range of time between A.D. 25–50—too wide to be chronologically useful.[7] That Paul participated in the stoning of Stephen, a doubtful detail that probably originated in Lukan redaction,[8] has little chronological relevance since the date of the stoning cannot be independently established.[9] Hence the safest place to begin is the date of the crucifixion.

## THE ALTERNATIVE DATES OF THE CRUCIFIXION

The date of Jesus' death is relevant for Pauline chronology because it provides a *terminus a quo* for the reckoning of the seventeen year span mentioned in Galatians between Paul's conversion, occurring sometime after the crucifixion, and Paul's participation in the Apostolic Conference. The conflicting fragments of evidence have led most scholars to date this event either in A.D. 30 or 33.[10] The arguments for the earlier option, set forth in studies by Strobel, Finegan, and Gunther are as follows.[11] Since the crucifixion took place on a Friday preceding the Passover that was celebrated on the 15th of Nisan, astronomical tables can be consulted to find the years in which this would have been possible. Assuming the correctness of this, the Johannine chronology (John 19:14, 31), Strobel and Finegan suggest that the choice is between Friday the third of April, 33, or Friday the seventh of April, 30.[12] The Synoptic chronology, with the 15th of Nisan Passover celebrated on a Thursday night, followed by the Friday crucifixion and a sabbath on the 17th (Mark 14:12–16; 15:42), would produce the options of A.D. 27 or 34,[13] neither of which appears probable when compared with other data from the life of Christ and the early church. Strobel opts for April 7, A.D. 30 because it correlates well with the Egyptian church calendar reflected in Clement of Alexandria, with the Montanist tradition, and with the early tradition of an 84 year Easter cycle associated with the Essene solar calendar.[14] He resolves the conflict between John and the Synoptics by asserting that the latter reflect a one day postponement of the Last Supper celebration by the early church, motivated by the eschatological expectations connected with the midnight of Passover. Substantiation is adduced from the argument of Claudius Apollinarius, the Talmudic traditions, the witness and practice of the early church and the church fathers, and finally in the critical analysis of Mark 14–15. Finegan resolves the same conflict between John and the Synoptics by asserting that the latter reckoned according to the older Israelite custom of a day running from sunrise to sunrise. In contrast, John presumably followed the later Jewish practice of reckoning a day from sundown to sundown. Thus the Synoptics had Jesus celebrate Passover on the evening of Thursday the 14th of Nisan; the crucifixion would thus have fallen on the 15th which began with the following sunrise. John followed the official reckoning that the 14th of Nisan began with sundown Thursday, so that it could rightfully be said that the crucifixion was on the "day of preparation" (John 19:31) before the Passover which would begin Friday night. It cannot be said that either of these harmonizing explanations is fully plausible.

With the evidence in John and the Synoptics so contradictory, the proper task is to discern which account is mistaken, rather than to look about for another ingenious harmonizing scheme. All of the current chronologies follow the Johannine dating scheme, despite the fact that Synoptic evidence is usually considered much more reliable. What seems to go unmentioned in pious treatments of this question[15] is that Mark's account of the Last Supper is internally inconsistent, because the traditional Passover foods and rituals were not prominent features of the original meal.[16] Redaction criticism suggests that Mark may have inserted Passover references as part of his effort to portray the Christian cult as a replacement of the Passover.[17] The reference in Rom. 14:6 to calendric celebrations implies a conflict over such questions as the status of Passover in the church with which Mark's Gospel is most closely associated.[18] The other Synoptics simply followed Mark in this mistaken identification of the last meal as a Passover celebration, thus causing the insuperable conflict in the chronology of Jesus' last week. One is forced therefore to rely entirely on the information in John, a regrettable state of affairs for the historian who would prefer to rest his case on the generally more dependable Synoptics.

Avoiding the unwelcome task of settling the conflict between John and the Synoptics, John Gunther argues for A.D. 30 on the premise of a three and a half year ministry commencing with the Jubilee Year on the first of Tishri, A.D. 26.[19] That Jesus' Nazareth sermon announced the Jubilee had been suggested by Strobel,[20] but this is far from certain.[21] Even if the Jubilee hypothesis were correct, the most reliable study of sabbatical cycles indicates that A.D. 27/28 rather than 26/27 is the year in question. The three and a half year ministry rests on Johannine rather than Synoptic evidence concerning the number of Passovers Jesus celebrated in Jerusalem (which is problematic in itself). But Gunther also argues for a conscious patterning after the prophecies in Dan. 9:24, 27, which seems quite improbable in light of Jesus' persistent refusal to speculate about the date of the eschatological fulfillment.[22] The reference to Elisha's Sidon ministry (Luke 4:23–25) does not really sustain Gunther's hypothesis, since the question of the duration of that ministry is not relevant to the context.[23] That the Parable of the Fig Tree (Luke 13:6–9) has precise allegorical reference to a three and a half year ministry is countered by all recent advances in parable criticism.[24] Gunther is able to correlate his dating scheme with the details about Jesus' birth (Luke 3:23) as well as with the Johannine detail about the 46th year of the temple (John 2:20),[25] but the reference to the "fifteenth year of Tiberius" (Luke 3:1–2) is played down as "indeterminate" and "ambiguous."[26] Actually the Tiberius date is an unequivocal reference to the commencement of Jesus' ministry in A.D. 28–29, as Richard Wellington Husband showed through an exhaustive analysis of inscriptive and papyri material from this period.[27]

The date of A.D. 33 for the crucifixion has been favored by Westberg, Husband, Fotheringham, Ogg, Reicke, Maier, and Botha.[28] Most recently Harold Hoehner has marshaled the evidence in a definitive statement of this position. Placing the birth of Jesus in 5/4 B.C.[29] and the commencement of his ministry at the end of the "fifteenth year of Tiberius" in the summer or autumn of A.D. 29,[30] he holds to a three and a half year ministry. largely on the basis of the three Passovers mentioned in John's Gospel and the conviction that the crucifixion took place in A.D. 33.[31] Placing the Passover meal/Last Supper on the Thursday evening of Nisan 14, he retains the traditional date of the crucifixion on the 15th, harmonizing the Synoptic and Johannine calendars by positing a "Galilean Method" of reckoning the day from sunrise to sunrise, which places the Passover on the day before the official Judean celebration.[32] This leads to A.D. 33 as the year of the crucifixion,[33] since there is unequivocal evidence that 15 Nisan fell on Friday,[34] and since it correlates well with the other details in Jesus' life. Hoehner rightly rejects the inclusion of considerations about the date of Paul's conversion that have led some scholars to reject the 33 date for the crucifixion.[35] His most cogent substantiation comes from an examination of Pilate's submissiveness to the demand for Barabbas' release and his sudden friendship with Herod Antipas. The pattern of anti–Semitic behavior that had marked Pilate's early tenure was consistent with the aims of his sponsor, the equestrian Sejanus, and had to be softened after the latter's execution in October, 31, by Tiberius. The need to appease the Jews in order to be a "friend of Caesar" (John 19:12) thus fits in with other actions reported by Josephus and Philo, indicating a change of policy after A.D. 32.[36] Since Herod Antipas had participated in the successful protest against Pilate's displaying of votive shields in the fall of that year,[37] it was only afterwards that cooperation in disposing of the troublesome case of Jesus could produce the reported friendship. "And Herod and Pilate became friends with each other that very day, for before this they had been at enmity with each other" (Luke 23:12).

The evidence seems to point therefore to April 3, A.D. 33, as the more probable date for the crucifixion. April 7, 30, is a slightly less probable option. Despite problems it may cause, the later date should probably be used in the construction of Pauline chronology.

## THE RESURRECTION APPEARANCES AND PAUL'S CONVERSION

In 1 Cor. 15:8, Paul speaks of his conversion as coming at the conclusion of the resurrection appearances: "Last of all, as to one untimely born, he appeared also to me." Since Paul is here describing the resurrection encounters in chronological sequence,[38] and since he assumes they belonged to a period of history ending with his own conversion,[39] it follows that one could calculate the date of the conversion from the span of the resurrection encounters. Adolf von Harnack confronted this question in 1912 and pointed out the relevance of the early Christian and Gnostic traditions concerning eighteen months of resurrection appearances.[40] The Ophites and the disciples of the Gnostic Ptolemaeus taught that Christ "conversed with his disciples for eighteen months after his resurrection from the dead."[41] The Ascension of Isaiah, a second century Christian work,[42] has an even more specific calculation of the period in question: "And when He (the Son of Man) shall have despoiled the angel of death, He will rise again on the third day and will remain on earth for five hundred and forty-five days."[43] The Apocryphon of James, a Christian or partially Gnostic work of the early second century,[44] refers to resurrection appearances for 550 days. Harnack argued that the eighteen month period was a historical recollection that probably derived from Pauline tradition.[45] Later research has confirmed his observation that Gnostic groups sometimes handed down independent and authentic strands of early Christian tradition.[46] The presence of the same datum in both orthodox and Gnostic works provides some substantiation of Harnack's claim that the eighteen month tradition is more authentic than either the Lukan reference to forty days before the Ascension (Acts 1:3)[47] or the third century Gnostic tradition of twelve years of secret instruction to the twelve disciples.[48]

It should nevertheless be acknowledged that the historical basis of this datum is extremely tenuous. It would be preposterous to base a chronology on such distant references. They would gain a minimal credibility only if they fit precisely into an already substantiated chronological scheme. The most one should conclude is that if the crucifixion took place on April 3 of A.D. 33, the conversion of Paul as the last of the resurrection appearances would fall on October 3 or 8, 34. If one chooses the earlier date for the crucifixion, the conversion would fall on October 7, 31, or using the 550 day tradition of the Apocryphon of James, on October 12, 31.

## PAUL'S ESCAPE FROM DAMASCUS

In 2 Cor. 11:32-33 Paul states that the ethnarch of King Aretas guarded Damascus to catch him, but that he escaped in a basket over the wall. Paul's reference to his return to Damascus in Gal. 1:17 would place this before his first Jerusalem visit (Gal. 1:18). It could not have occurred after this, because Paul explicitly states that he went to Syria and Cilicia rather than Arabia (Gal. 1:21), which leads Alfred Suhl to conclude that he was forced to shift his residence from Damascus because of the political difficulties experienced there.[49] Acts 9:23-25 appears to describe the same event and confirms that it occurred just prior to Paul's first trip to Jerusalem. Even if one chose to place the escape earlier in the three year period between Paul's conversion and the first Jerusalem journey,[50] the limited range of possibilities remains chronologically useful.

The absolute *terminus ad quem* for this trip is provided by the fact that Aretas IV died between A.D. 38–40. This is reckoned on the basis that his reign probably began in 9 B.C. (Josephus, *Antiquities*, XVI, 294) and that the numerous inscriptions concerning his reign as well as his coins cease with the 48th year.[51] The flexibility in the ancient dating system allows his death to be placed in A.D. 38[52] or 40,[53] but Gutschmid's analysis of the sequence of events before and after Aretas' accession to the throne makes it probable that his 48th year fell in the year A.D. 39.[54] The question is whether the period of Aretas' surveillance over Damascus can be more closely dated to provide a narrow margin in which to set a portion of the Pauline chronology.

Kirsopp Lake,[55] Ernst Haenchen,[56] and others have argued that Aretas never controlled the city of Damascus itself, but had some of his men watch the city gates from the outside. If this were so, the establishment of a useful *terminus a quo* would be impossible. So the first task is to examine the plausibility of this argument. The theory that some of Aretas' caravaneers guarded the city gates is as difficult to reconcile with the political and geographic situation of the city as it is with Paul's account in 2 Corinthians. It is conceivable that a small force might unobtrusively guard the gates of a small city without the knowledge and approval of a Roman garrison. But in the case of a large city like Damascus, with seven fortified gates,[57] set in the midst of a large and heavily vegetated oasis, this would have required a redoubtable force. It would have amounted to a virtual state of siege. This would have been quite impossible without the express approval of the Roman garrison that controlled not only the city but also the surrounding country for many miles in every direction.[58] Furthermore, the gates of major frontier cities such as Damascus during the Roman period were designed to control the access roads to the city. Caravaneers would not carelessly lie in ambush on a road within close proximity to the towers. An analysis of 2 Cor. 11:32f. likewise indicates the implausibility of the caravaneer hypothesis. Going over a city wall in a basket makes sense only if the danger is within the city; it would be absurd to drop over the wall into the hands of an encircling force that could not harm one within the city itself. A force exercising effective control over the seven gates of a more or less circular city would in fact be far more apt to see a basket being lowered over the wall than would the men guarding the gates from the inside. Haenchen's second argument is that Aretas would have ordered a police raid to apprehend Paul if he had actually controlled the city. But was Paul really important enough at that time to warrant the unusual measure of a police dragnet when a simple watch at the gates was assumed to be sufficient? Furthermore the mixed constitution of the so-called "free" Roman city in the East did not necessarily give the supervising client king unlimited police powers. The supervision was a limited one in cities such as the Decapolis—among which Damascus was occasionally reckoned—[59] and it related mainly to foreign affairs, commerce, and taxation.[60]

These considerations have led most specialists to assume that Aretas IV gained some supervisory control over Damascus itself.[61] In all probability the Nabataean king exercised political control through one of his sheiks.[62] The question which remains is when such control began.[63]

Although Damascus was able at times to maintain its independence as a city with a substantial surrounding territory,[64] even becoming the capital of an independent kingdom at the turn of the first century B.C. under a son of Antiochus VIII, its strategic position commanding the trade routes to the East caused it to come under the fluctuating control of the larger powers. Occasionally the Nabataeans succeeded in controlling it.[65] Even after it became a part of the Syrian province under Roman control, they did not give up their interest in its importance as a station on their trade route.[66] But during Tiberius' reign it is extremely doubtful whether Aretas would have been granted even nominal control over Damascus.

The official policy of the emperor regarding the eastern frontier was to discourage client kingdoms in favor of regularly organized provinces such as Syria.[67] This was probably the major reason Tiberius favored Antipas over Aretas in the border conflict around A.D. 36. At any event when the emperor dispatched the Syrian governor Vitellius with two legions on the punitive expedition against Aretas in late 36 or early 37, the column did not advance through Damascus but went by ship to Ptolemais and then crossed lower Galilee on the way to Petra.[68] Vitellius himself proceeded by way of Jerusalem where he heard of Tiberius' death, probably at the end of March or early April, 37 (Tiberius died March 16). This brought the punitive expedition to a halt, but it is apparent from the attack route that Aretas was not in control of Rome's valuable city of Damascus. Otherwise the recapture of Damascus would have been an immediate strategic necessity for Vitellius.[69] Such considerations also make it implausible that Aretas could have forcibly wrested control of Damascus from the Romans during this period or at some earlier date as some have suggested. The four Roman legions stationed in Syria[70] would have been more than enough to discourage such a foolhardy attempt on the part of Aretas, who was after all a client king of the Roman Empire. Nor can the oft-mentioned lack of Roman coins in Damascus between the years A.D. 34 and 62[71] be advanced as a conclusive argument that the Nabataeans had control from an early date. The city of Damascus has not been thoroughly excavated and the few coins of any description which have been catalogued are insufficient to provide a valid argument. There is no avoiding the conclusion that up until the death of Tiberius, Nabataean control of Damascus was highly unlikely.

The radical change in frontier policy during the reign of Gaius, on the other hand, provided a setting in which Nabataean control was very much to be expected. Reversing the policies of his predecessor, Gaius reestablished a system of client kings in the east[72] and parceled out substantial sections of the province of Syria to various princes. In A.D. 37 Commagene, which for twenty years had been a part of Syria, became an independent kingdom for Gaius' friend, Antiochus. In the following year the area of Iturea was given to the native prince Sohaemus (cf. Dio Cassius 59:12). In 37 and 49 Agrippa received increases of territory in Transjordan. The transfer of Damascus to Nabataean control indicated by 2 Cor. 11:32f. probably also occurred during the early years of Caligula's administration.[73] This is substantiated by the fact that the new emperor refrained from confirming Vitellius' orders to proceed with the punitive expedition against Aretas. Balsdon notes that although Vitellius waited for such an order, ". . . no confirmation came; on the contrary Gaius adopted a friendly attitude towards Aretas. No doubt he remembered the favors which Aretas had once shown to Germanicus."[74] Manfred Lindner concurs in suggesting that the emperor transferred Damascus to Nabataean control at this time.[75] Since the negotiations about the transfer could scarcely have been completed before the summer of A.D. 37,[76] this provides a *terminus a quo* for Paul's escape from the ethnarch of Aretas. Paul's escape occurred sometime within the two year span until the death of Aretas in A.D. 39. This is a datum whose historical solidity is capable of anchoring a chronology.

## THE RELEVANCE OF AGRIPPA'S DEATH

The death of Herod Agrippa at the feast in Caesarea in early March, A.D. 44,[77] has been used by John J. Gunther, Ferdinand Hahn, and Alfred Suhl as a means to date the Apostolic Conference and Paul's conversion.[78] Hahn follows Eduard Schwartz[79] in arguing that since Agrippa persecuted the church shortly before his death, killing James and John and causing Peter to flee Jerusalem, the Apostolic Conference attended by Peter and John must have taken place in the winter of A.D. 43–44. This argument contains several problematic assumptions and requires a juggling of evidence in regard to the date of Paul's conversion which took place seventeen years before the conference. That John was martyred with his brother James is denied by Acts 12:2 and sustained only on the basis of Papias and the fourth century Syrian tradition,[80] both of which are obviously dependent upon the gospel tradition that the sons of Zebedee would be "baptized with Jesus' baptism" through martyrdom (Mark 10:39).[81] That Peter was banned from Jerusalem after the death of Agrippa cannot be proven by the simple reference to his having departed "to another place" (Acts 12:17) after escaping from prison. Furthermore, since Peter was imprisoned at Passover time which came several weeks after the death of Agrippa in the year 44,[82] the latest possible date for the persecution of the church would be the spring of 43. This means that the Apostolic Conference would have taken place in the winter of 42–43 and that the seventeen year span between the conference and Paul's conversion, even if compressed into fifteen years according to Hahn's hypothesis, would set the conversion considerably before the most probable date for the crucifixion. Because of this compression, Hahn is forced to reject the evidence concerning the Passover in Acts 12:3 in order to set the conference in the winter of 43–44. Such data manipulation would be questionable even if the arguments regarding the death of John and the permanent exile of Peter were valid.

Although Agrippa's persecution of the church the year before his death in A.D. 44 is a well-established date in the history of the early church, it throws no particular light on the problem of Pauline chronology.

## THE PROBLEM OF THE FAMINE-RELIEF VISIT

Acts 11:27–30 reports a world-wide famine in the reign of Claudius which caused the Antioch church to send Paul and Barnabas with relief funds to the stricken church in Judea. The problem with this report is that Paul in Galatians 1–2 categorically denies having made a trip to Jerusalem between the time of his acquaintance journey three years after his conversion and the date of the Apostolic Conference. Joachim Jeremias[83] and others have argued that the famine expedition and the trip for the Apostolic Conference were one and the same thing. Since Paul mentions nothing about such a double purpose for the journey in Gal. 2:1ff.—and one would think that a reference to the relief project would be a natural opportunity for him to demonstrate both good will and independence— one hesitates to accept such a suggestion.

It would be more consistent with the evidence to accept Robert W. Funk's hypothesis that Luke placed an Antiochene report of a famine visit in Paul's earlier ministry where it does not belong.[84] This displacement helps close out the Antioch phase of Paul's activities and avoids reintroducing Barnabas in Acts 24 where the relief journey probably belongs. Furthermore it allows Luke to connect the offering with a famine and the Agabus prophecy instead of with the gentile conflict and the subsequent agreement to "remember the poor" in Jerusalem (Gal. 2:10). At any rate, the evidence indicates that Paul did not participate in a relief expedition to Jerusalem either during or prior to the Apostolic Conference. Thus, dating the famine on the basis of Josephus' references (*Ant.* XX, 97–104) to the periods of Cuspius Fadus (44–46) and Tiberius Alexander (46–48) does nothing to advance the search for dates relevant to Pauline chronology.[85]

## THE RELEVANCE OF THE "WRATH" AND THE "RESTRAINER"

In 1 Thess. 2:16 there is a reference to an act of judgment which Paul felt had befallen his Jewish adversaries: "The wrath has caught up with them at last." There is an apocalyptic implication in the phrase "at last," that the wrath is being visited ahead of time in some historical catastrophe.[86] Buck and Taylor argue that there "is really only one event in this period that completely satisfies the requirements of the case. That is the famine that occurred in Judea in the year 46."[87] Two points are advanced in support of this: the famine was a disaster of great magnitude, and in Rom. 8:35 Paul lists famine as an apocalyptic woe. But when one turns to the literature on this question, it is immediately apparent that several equally plausible theories have been suggested. The disaster may have been Claudius' expulsion of the Jews from Rome,[88] the insurrection of Theudas (Acts 5:36),[89] or some event expected in the near future.[90] It would be possible to make a choice between these alternatives if one were certain of the precise date of writing, but there is no conclusive way to infer the date of writing from the reference to the disaster. 1 Thess. 2:16 lacks the kind of specificity required for chronological usefulness.

A similarly vague conclusion results when one examines Buck and Taylor's argument that the one who "restrains" the "man of lawlessness" in 2 Thess. 2:3–7 was the Emperor Claudius who succeeded the demented Caligula in A.D. 41.[91] On grounds of Paul's reminder about his teaching on this point during his short Thessalonian ministry (2 Thess. 2:5), they date his visit as ending "before Caligula's death, or at least before Claudius had restored order," no later than January, 41.[92] They date the writing of 2 Thessalonians on the basis of the reference in 2:2 to the parousia already having come, suggesting the Thessalonians may have applied the three and a half year period of the Abomination of Desolation in Dan. 7:25 and 12:11–13. There is, of course, not a shred of evidence that the Thessalonians actually did this, or indeed that this predominately gentile congregation even knew of Daniel.[93] Nevertheless Buck and Taylor conclude "The date of II Thessalonians, therefore, can be fixed. It cannot have been written before early September of the year 44, for the 1,335 days were not up until then. It can hardly have been written very long after that time either, for it deals with matters that were still a subject of urgent debate. It may safely be placed, therefore, in the fall of the year 44."[94]

This ingenious construction of an "absolute date"[95] rests on an interpretation of some notoriously vague references in 2 Thessalonians, following a procedure which does not even refer to the bewildering array of exegetical options.[96] The "lawless one" has been identified as Belial,[97] a false prophet within the church,[98] a superhuman figure coming out of Judaism,[99] a metahistorical figure or type symbolizing opposition to God's reign,[100] or a strictly human deceiver who plays the anti–Christ role in the drama of the end time.[101] As far as the identification with an emperor is concerned, the most recent commentary notes that "unlike Dan. 11:36 the figure of 2 Thess. 2:3f. shows no 'royal' characteristics and there is no reason, if he is historical, to think of him as 'royal.' "[102] The "restrainer" has been identified in ways whose plausibility equals or exceeds that of Buck and Taylor's theory; for example: as an angelic force which binds Satan,[103] the gospel preaching[104] or Paul himself as a gospel advocate,[105] an evil person or power who holds greater evils at bay,[106] the false prophet "seized" with the message that the Day of the Lord had already come,[107] or God himself who "delays" the parousia.[108] Without the elimination of these alternative viewpoints and a detailed exegetical demonstration of the superiority of the Caligula/Claudius theory, it is difficult to view Buck and Taylor's use of this material as convincing.[109]

## PAUL'S ENCOUNTER WITH SERGIUS PAULUS

In the account of the first missionary expedition there is a reference to a Sergius Paulus, the proconsul of Cyprus (Acts 13:6–12). Unfortunately the efforts to date the tenure of this official have failed. The inscription found at Soloi has a postscript referring to a governmental reorganization "in the proconsulship of Paulus."[110] The inscription is dated in the 13th year, and even if the point of reference could be agreed upon, no more than a *terminus ad quem* would be established because the reorganization occurred some time before the other events alluded to in the inscription. If the 13th year were reckoned from the establishment of Cyprus as a senatorial province in 22 B.C., the postscript would refer to Paulus Fabius Maximus who was consul in 11 B.C.[111] If the 13th year were dated from Claudius' reign, the *terminus ad quem* would be A.D. 53. Although this does not conflict with the usual dating of the Cyprus expedition in the 30s or 40s, it provides no basis for a more precise dating.[112] The inscriptions found by Ramsay and Calder in South Galatia which refer to the family of Sergius Paulus can be dated in the first through third centuries A.D. but otherwise provide no corroboration for the reference in Acts.[113]

## THE EDICT OF CLAUDIUS

Acts 18:2 reports that when Paul arrived in Corinth he encountered Aquila and Priscilla who had recently come from Rome because of Claudius' edict banning the Christians from that city. Suetonius records an edict of this sort in his *Life of Claudius* XXV: "*Iudaios impulsore*

*Chresto adsidue tumultuantes Roma expulit.*" The extensive scholarly debate over this edict[114] is due in part to the seemingly conflicting tendencies in Claudius' religious policies. Momigliano devotes considerable attention to this issue in his biography of Claudius,[115] stressing that the emperor was torn between the desire to restore rights to the Jews and at the same time prevent public disorders and open propagandizing in Rome. In A.D. 41 he published an edict restoring to Jews in the entire empire the civil rights abrogated by Gaius, an edict similar to the one affirming rights to the Jews in Alexandria. But in the same year there is a notation by Dio Cassius (LX, 6, 6) that the large number of Jews in Rome made their expulsion impossible, so that Claudius forbade their assembly. The implication is that some public disorder or infraction of Roman regulations raised the question of whether all the Jews should not be expelled and that this impractical idea was dropped.[116] Momigliano finds no conflict here because the Jewish right to worship in the Roman Empire as a whole did not give them the right to disobey the particular regulations of individual cities. In the case of Rome, proselytizing was punishable by the magistrates charged with the protection of Roman religion. The specific cause for the disturbance in A.D. 41 is unknown; there is no evidence it was caused by Christian agitation.

The expulsion mentioned by Suetonius probably refers to riots which occurred within the Jewish community toward the end of the 40s. It is widely assumed that the "Chrestus" in question was Christ, who Suetonius thought must have been present to provoke such a tumult.[117] In this instance it was probably the Christian instigators who were banned. Scramuzza concludes from the evidence that the tumult reflected a ". . . splitting of the Roman synagogue into two factions, that of the orthodox and that of the Christian believers. Claudius . . . expelled the leaders of the Christian sect, but allowed the orthodox to retain their traditional mode of worship, although forbidding them to hold any religious assembly until the excitement cooled off."[118] That Acts 18:2 refers to "all the Jews" being expelled from Rome seems to fit the hyperbolic sense which *pas* sometimes bears in Acts and elsewhere.[119] It was all the agitators rather than all 50,000 Jews in Rome who were banned, thus bringing leaders like Priscilla and Aquila to places like Corinth.

Since the Suetonius reference to the edict of Claudius is not dated, the only way to utilize it chronologically is by means of the reference by the fifth century church historian Orosius that it occurred in Claudius' ninth year.[120] This would place it between the 25th of January, A.D. 49 and the

24th of January, A.D. 50.[121] Considerable debate has been provoked by the fact that Orosius erroneously attributed this datum to Josephus.[122] Harnack showed that Orosius did not utilize Josephus, deriving his information from an expanded Chronicle of Hieronymus.[123] He concluded that the "ninth year of Claudius" was a reliable ancient tradition even though its precise origin was obscure. Despite the sometimes questionable accuracy of Orosius,[124] this conclusion is corroborated by the striking correlation with the arrival of Paul as reckoned on the basis of the Gallio inscription.[125] Both sources lead to the conclusion that the encounter between Paul and the two Roman expatriates took place in A.D. 49–50. Reckoning several months for travel from Rome and resettlement in Corinth, the encounter must have taken place sometime between the spring of A.D. 49 and the spring of A.D. 50.[126] The corroboration from the Gallio inscription makes this a datum of crucial significance in the construction of a chronology.

## THE GALLIO PROCONSULSHIP

Acts 18:12 reports that when Gallio was proconsul of Achaia, the Jews brought Paul before the tribunal. The usual deduction is that Paul's opponents made use of the chance to get a fresh hearing as soon as the new proconsul came to office.[127] If this could be proven, a knowledge of the date Gallio acceded to office would give a precise date from which to estimate the beginning of Paul's Corinthian ministry as well as the date of his departure from Corinth. But as Wendt pointed out, there is actually nothing in the wording of Acts 18:12, which requires so precise a conclusion.[128] Haacker has argued persuasively that the hearing could have occurred anytime during Gallio's term of office.[129] Nevertheless, the dating of Gallio's term of office will provide an important set of time limits for Paul's Corinthian ministry.

Fortunately there are various means of determining the date Gallio arrived in Achaia. In the middle of the last century, long before the discovery of the Gallio inscription at Delphi, Wieseler reckoned the date on the basis that Gallio's brother, Seneca, could have procured the office for him only after his return from exile in A.D. 49. Thus Gallio was consul in Rome in 50 and was appointed proconsul of Achaia in 51.[130] An important biography of Claudius written in 1858 arrived at the same conclusion on the basis of data concerning the imperial establishment;[131] a reconstruction of Gallio's prior and subsequent career concurs.[132] The remarkable inscription found at Delphi shortly after the turn of the last century, recording a case in which the Emperor Claudius decided in Delphi's favor during the period Gallio was in Corinth, points in the same direction.[133] Gallio's name is mentioned in the extant portions of the inscription and even the date of Claudius' letter is legible. It was written during the period of his 26th Acclamation as Imperator. On the basis of other inscriptions and imperial data, it is clear that this acclamation fell between January 25 and August 1, A.D. 52, very probably in the spring of that year.[134] On this basis Adolph Deissmann concluded that "the letter of Claudius to Delphi was written between . . . the beginning of 52 and August 1, 52."[135] This judgment has since been accepted by most other scholars as well.[136] The conclusion is not altered by the subsequent discovery of five additional fragments,[137] or by the resultant possibility that the letter was addressed by an imperial bureaucrat in Claudius' name to Gallio's immediate successor.[138] The reference in the inscription to Gallio's disposition of the case and the instructions to the new proconsul lead Plassart to place the letter in the closing months of Gallio's tenure, in May or June, A.D. 52.[139]

Considerable attention has been devoted to the question of how long before this date Gallio's term of office would have begun. During Tiberius' reign the date for accession to office in the senatorial provinces was July 1.[140] Some scholars have inferred a May 1 accession date on the basis of references in Dio Cassius, but Mommsen is probably right in suggesting Claudius ordered the April 1 departure from Rome for provincial office holders in order to ensure a smooth governmental transition in midsummer (Dio Cassius LX, 11, 6), a measure he later softened by setting the date in mid–April (Dio Cassius LX, 17, 3). In all probability the standard date for the transition remained July 1, which corresponds well with the fact that the usual term of office consisted of six months in each of two calendar years.[141] Now if Gallio arrived in Corinth July 1, 52, he would scarcely have had time to hear an important case, come to a decision, hear an appeal and send the report on to Rome for a ruling before the absolute deadline of August 1, 52. Indeed, Ernst Haenchen has convincingly shown that such an appeal process would have been impossible even within a three month period, thus rendering improbable even the possibility that Gallio may have acceded to office as early as May 1, 52.[142] If the Plassart dating of the letter is correct, such a possibility is definitely excluded. Gallio must have taken office the year before, his term running from July 1, A.D. 51 until July 1, A.D. 52. This assumes that the custom of holding office for only one year in the senatorial provinces held sway in this case.[143] Deissmann noted that Gallio contracted an illness from the Corinthian climate (Seneca, Ep. Mor. 104:1) and suggested that he may not even have remained at duty for the entire year.[144] At any rate a longer period in office is rendered improbable by such illness, and the customary maximum length of one year stands until there is evidence to the contrary. One is forced to conclude that Gallio entered office around July 1, 51 and that Paul appeared before him sometime during the twelve month period ending with July 1, A.D. 52.[145] The high level of certainty that can be claimed for this conclusion makes it the pivotal date in the construction of Pauline chronology.

## THE REBEL FROM EGYPT

Acts 21:38 reports that while Paul was being arrested in Jerusalem the Roman tribune asked him if he were not "the Egyptian who recently stirred up a revolt and led the four thousand men of the Sicarii out into the wilderness." Josephus mentions this Egyptian rebel and describes how Felix struck quickly to scatter his threatening force.[146] Since Josephus discussed this event after the death of Claudius (*Ant.* XX, 158ff.) in October, 54, Paul's arrest in Jerusalem could not have taken place before Pentecost, 55.[147] In fact the years 56 or 57 would be more probable since the territorial changes under Nero (*Ant.* XX 158ff.), Felix's campaigns against the Zealots and his capture of their leader, Eleazar (*Ant.* XX, 160ff.), and the machinations leading to the assassination of the high priest Jonathan (*Ant.* XX, 163ff.) all took place before the Egyptian affair.[148] The conclusions are that the earliest possible *terminus a quo* for Paul's arrest is A.D. 55, while the probable *terminus a quo* is A.D. 56. Ben Zion Wacholder's analysis of the correlation of messianic movements with sabbatical cycles confirms this conclusion. He suggests "Nisan of 56" as "the likely date of the Egyptian prophet . . ," which brings the probable *terminus a quo* to April, 56.[149]

## THE HEARINGS BEFORE FELIX AND FESTUS

Despite the skepticism of theologians such as Ernst Haenchen, the judicial details relating to Paul's appearance before Felix and Festus are so accurate that solid historical information must have been available to the author. Roman historian A. N. Sherwin-White summarizes his extensive analysis as follows: "The account of the trial before Festus and Felix is then sufficiently accurate in all its details. In its references to *provocatio* it is in accord with what is otherwise known of the practice in the first century A.D. What is equally important is the fact that the author does not confuse *provocatio* with the procedure of the late Empire known as *appelatio,* which is a very different business. In this the author has the advantage over some modern critics."[150] The result is that one can place some reliance on the reference in Acts 25:1 to Festus' accession as a datum in Pauline chronology. It can be accurately dated using extra-biblical evidence. Both Tacitus, (*Ann.* XII, 54) and Josephus (*Bell.* II, 232ff.) refer to Festus' predecessor, Felix, though unfortunately in a conflicting fashion. Haenchen solved this conflict by demonstrating that Tacitus misunderstood his source of information in thinking that Cumanus and Felix were procurators at the same time over a divided Palestine.[151] In reality Cumanus was Felix's predecessor in the same office. On grounds that his account is more specific and generally more dependable in such questions, I accept Josephus' view that Felix was appointed by Claudius after the latter had arbitrated over the border conflict between the Samaritans and the Jews in the last years of Cumanus' term. This hearing before Claudius took place some time after the Jewish delegation arrived in Rome, having been sent from Caesarea around Passover time in A.D. 52 (*Bell.* II, 243f.). Thus the best assumption is that Felix was appointed some time later that year and arrived in Palestine in the autumn of 52 or the spring of 53.[152]

When Festus replaced Felix as procurator is more difficult to determine. Some NT exegetes date this in A.D. 54–56[153] while historians tend to place it in A.D. 58–61.[154] The earlier date is reckoned from Josephus' statement that Felix's brother, Pallas, saved him from disgrace or censure at the time of his replacement by Festus (*Ant.* XX, 182). Since Pallas lost his office as financial secretary to the emperor in the latter part of the year 55, the assumption is that he could not have assisted his brother after this date. The later dating of Festus' accession is the result of working out the progression of Roman procurators in the years prior to the Jewish War. The war broke out in May, 66,[155] which was in the second year of the Procurator Gessius Florus (Jos. *Ant.* XX, 252). The last procurator was thus in office from summer 64 until May, 66. The previous procurator, Albinus, was in office in 62 when the prophecy of Jesus, Son of Ananias, took place (Jos. *Bell.* VI, 301ff.), and most historians assume that he came to office in the summer of that year. Since Felix came to office in 52 or 53, there are about ten years which must be divided between him and Festus.[156] From *Bell.* II, 247–276 one gains the impression that Felix was procurator during most of this period. Josephus reports a number of incidents which occurred under Felix, while devoting one sentence to describing Festus' activities in very general terms. In the parallel account, *Ant.* XX, 185ff., Josephus reports in less general terms that Festus sent his troops to put down a rebellion in the desert. Then he relates the account of the conflict between Agrippa and the temple authorities which came to its climax under Festus. Even in this longer account of Festus' activities one gains the impression that he was in office a relatively short time.

A decisive clue is Josephus' remark that the incidents which occurred under Felix took place during Nero's reign (*Bell.* II, 250–270). If Felix had been replaced in the summer of A.D. 55, all these incidents must have taken place in a nine month period after Nero came to power in October, 54. A close reading of Josephus reveals that such compression is not possible. Plooij deduced, for example, on the basis of the reference to the Egyptian rebel (Acts 21:38; Jos. *Ant.* XX, 8:6) that Felix must have remained in office at least until the summer of 57.[157] It was under the pressure of such considerations that Harnack felt impelled to move the change of administration from A.D. 55 to 56,[158] which would imply that Tacitus had been mistaken about the date of Pallas' fall from office. But granting the evidence its due weight, one cannot avoid the conclusion that Felix ended his term as procurator of Judea after his brother was relieved from his office by Nero in the winter of 55.

This necessitates a reexamination of the assumption that Pallas could not have helped his brother after this date. It is interesting that no specialist in Roman history has advanced such a view. As the *Cambridge Ancient History* makes clear,[159] Nero had no personal antipathy against Pallas. The dismissal served first to weaken the position of Agrippina who had used Pallas to gain her own ends (cf. Tac. *Ann.* XIII, 14); a second factor was Seneca's ambition to reshape the fiscal policy, a purpose which could only be attained by replacing Pallas, who was the chief architect of the previous financial administration (cf. Tac. *Ann.* XIII, 2). Pallas left office surrounded by a crowd of servants as was fitting for an honored official. He even took the oath which hitherto only high magistrates had taken, showing he had done nothing against the law (cf. Tac. *Ann.* 14). In the following year he was fully exonerated from a charge of conspiracy and even succeeded in having the state treasury books which contained damaging evidence against him burned by the court (*Ann.* XIII, 23). Clearly Pallas' influence was not yet exhausted, and its source is obvious: his riches were literally proverbial (Juv. I, 109). As a former slave he could scarcely have been granted the senatorial *ornamenta praetoria* and a public monument acclaiming his services (Plin. *ep.* VIII, 6; VII, 29) unless certain senators had harbored hopes of a sizable legacy out of this ill–amassed fortune. In the end, when Nero had him poisoned in A.D. 62, he did so out of impatience that the old man lived so long holding onto his money (Tac. *Ann.* XIV, 65). Dio reports that Nero killed him out of greed for his 400 million sesterces (Dio Cassius, LXII, 14:3). In short, up until the year 62, Pallas had the influence of an immensely rich bachelor from whom senators and even the emperor had hoped to receive legacies. There is little doubt that such influence would suffice to thwart a Jewish delegation complaining about the behavior of his brother.[160] Thus the early dating of Festus' succession of Felix is not only incompatible with Josephus' account of the activities of the procurators prior to the Jewish War, but also its main supposition—that Pallas could not have helped his brother after 55—is invalid.

One is therefore forced to decide between the later dates for Festus' entrance into office. The date of 56 provided by the Latin version of Eusebius[161] is rendered improbable by the reference in Acts 21:38 to the Egyptian rebel whom the tribune confused with Paul at the time of his arrest in Jerusalem. Josephus implies that the rebel appeared during Nero's reign, i.e., sometime after October 13, 54 (*Ant.* XX, 158ff., 169ff.). If Paul was apprehended on the first Pentecost after this date and imprisoned for two years until Festus took office, this would bring one at least to A.D. 57, thereby eliminating the Eusebius date. It has also been suggested that the "two years" in Acts 24:27 referred to the period Felix held office, rather than to the period of Paul's incarceration.[162] But I would concur with Weiss' reasoning that Acts 24:27 would not refer to the length of Felix's administration unless its beginning had been specifically mentioned in Acts.[163] The topic of Acts, after all, is Paul's imprisonment rather than the history of Roman provincial administration. So with the *terminus ad quem* of A.D. 60–61, approximately one year before Festus' death in office, there is a choice of three to four years for the date of Paul's hearing before Festus. Since Felix was in office "for many years" before Paul first appeared before him (Acts 24:10), and since the activities reported during his administration seem to require at least seven or eight years, I conclude that he was replaced by Festus in the summer of either 59 or 60.[164] If Plooij and Caird are right, the year 59 is the more probable of the two; they argue that Eusebius mistakenly reckoned

Festus' accession in the tenth year of Agrippa II from the year 45 rather than the year 50 when Agrippa actually took office. Thus, according to the source Eusebius was using, presumably Justus of Tiberias, the first year of Festus' procuratorship was in the year 59.[165] The coins minted in Palestine during the fifth year of Nero (A.D. 58–59) also correlate well with this date.[166]

## THE ENCOUNTER WITH ANANIAS THE HIGH PRIEST

When Paul was being questioned before the Sanhedrin during his final visit to Jerusalem, he was censured by Ananias the high priest (Acts 23:1-5; 24:1). Ananias, the son of Nebedaios, was appointed high priest in A.D. 47[167] and served until he was temporarily released from office when he was sent in chains to Claudius after the strife with the Samaritans in 52 (Jos. *Ant.* XX, 125–133). The emperor promptly ruled in favor of the Jewish delegation and presumably they returned home when Felix was sent as the new procurator, in late 52 or early 53 (*Ant.* XX, 134–137). Some believe that Ananias was replaced as high priest in 52,[168] but most authorities contend that he remained in office until replaced by Agrippa II in A.D. 59 (Jos. *Ant.* XX, 179).[169] Finally he was killed by the Zealots at the beginning of the Jewish War. His tenure in office thus spans the years from A.D. 53 when he returned from Rome until 59 when he was replaced. Paul encountered him sometime during this period.

## PAUL'S ARRIVAL IN ROME

The *terminus ad quem* for Paul's arrival in Rome has been reckoned by Wieseler and Plooij on the basis of the Western Text's reference to the delivery of Paul and his fellow prisoners to a single prefect (Acts 28:16).[170] The last single office holder in this position was Burrus who died in January, 62. After this Nero appointed two men to the position. This would imply that the summer of 61 is the last possible date for arrival in Rome. Clemen objected that the singular here may refer simply to the particular prefect who took responsibility for the prisoners.[171] But Plooij showed through parallels in Pliny *ep.* X, 57 and Philostratus *Vit. Soph.* II, 32 that the customary usage after A.D. 62 refers to the office of prefect in the plural form. Certainty is not possible at this point, especially in light of the generally secondary nature of the Western Text of Acts.[172] The most one can conclude is that A.D. 61 is a fairly likely *terminus ad quem* for Paul's arrival in Rome.

## THE QUESTION OF A SPANISH MISSION
## AND THE DEATH OF PAUL

The evidence concerning the end of Paul's life has been deeply entangled with the question of the authorship of the Pastoral Epistles.[173] The references to the "first defense" in 2 Tim. 4:16 and his "rescue" in 4:17 have led scholars ever since the time of Eusebius to conclude that Paul was released after the two year imprisonment mentioned in Acts 28:30.[174] Since there is so little likelihood that the Pastorals are genuine, this evidence should be rigorously excluded from our consideration. Most of the other evidence cited on this question appears to be highly problematic. The references in Eusebius, Jerome, and the apocryphal Acts of Peter reflect the secondary combination of references in the Pastorals with Rom. 15:24.[175] The reference to Paul's journey to Spain in the Muratori Canon appears even more remote.[176] The church history of Spain begins with the second century and contains no "positive proof" of a Pauline visit.[177] The only reliable extra–canonical source that bears directly on this question is Clement's Epistle to the Corinthians. However, the references to Paul's "exile" and his reaching the "farthest bounds of the West" are vaguely formulated and do not explicitly demand the Spanish hypothesis.[178] The degree to which even Clement is influenced by knowledge of Rom. 15:24 is difficult to determine, and unfortunately he provides no precise chronological details when describing Paul's martyrdom. Although it is mentioned prior to Clement's description of the Neronian persecution, it is hazardous to draw precise chronological conclusions except that it suggests a likely *terminus ad quem* shortly after July, 64.[179]

The decisive evidence is in the final verses of the Book of Acts: "And he lived there two whole years . . . preaching . . . quite openly and unhindered" (Acts 28:30–31). None of the suggestions about Paul's release after the two year imprisonment stand up under close examination.[180] A consideration of the redactional evidence suggests that Luke intended to conclude his work on the most positive note he could find, and that the prediction of martyrdom he included in the farewell speech to the Ephesian elders (Acts 20:24, 38) was intended to indicate what occurred at the end of the two year period.[181] In all probability the beheading which "ancient, reliable tradition" placed on the Ostian Road[182] took place at this time.

A *terminus a quo* for the end of this two year period can be established on the basis of details from Nero's administration. While Nero's early years were marked by exemplary judicial fairness and an absence of treason trials, Momigliano describes the "increasingly suspicious temper of the government" after A.D. 60 and the restoration of treason trials two years later.[183] Early in A.D. 62, when the sensible and efficient Burrus died and Seneca was dismissed, the law of *maiestas* was restored.[184] An important observation in this connection is that in an apology Luke appears to have created (Acts 25:8), the apostle defends himself against precisely this charge.[185] This in all likelihood reflects the actual charge on which Paul was executed,[186] a penalty that probably would not have been enacted prior to A.D. 62. A further contributing factor in the same year was Nero's marriage to Poppaea. Since she was a powerful friend of the Jews,[187] her ascendency would have had a decidedly negative effect on Paul's case. Since both the restoration of the treason and sedition laws and the marriage to Poppaea took place in A.D. 62, this year constitutes the probable *terminus a quo* for the tragic conclusion of Paul's two year imprisonment.[188] An even more precise reckoning is possible when one calculates backwards from June 9, 62, the date of Octavia's execution, to her banishment to the island of Pandateria, and her earlier exile to a country estate in Campania after the divorce from Nero.[189] The divorce and Nero's marriage to Poppaea must have occurred in the spring.[190] The probable date-range for the execution of Paul thus runs from spring, 62, to August, 64.

# CHAPTER III

# THE INTERNALLY ASCERTAINABLE DATE-RANGES AND TIME-SPANS

There are a number of dates and time-spans visible in the letters and Acts that cannot be verified by reference to external history. Some of these can be determined on the basis of astronomical, geographic, or seasonal data. For the most part the information thus gained is chronologically useful only when correlated with a framework created on the basis of other data. Such information can provide useful positive and negative functions, rendering implausible those hypotheses which prove contradictory, and confirming the workability of hypotheses that successfully incorporate them. A methodical approach demands, however, that these dates and time–spans be determined entirely on the basis of the evidence in each case, without regard to the potential chronological consequences.

## PAUL'S DEPARTURE FROM TROAS

In Acts 16:11 there is a precise description of Paul's journey from Troas to Philippi. In this portion of the "we–account" it is stated that the travelers made the journey by ship in two days' time. It took one day from Troas to Samothrace, where they anchored overnight, and one more day to Neapolis, the harbor of Philippi. This is very good time for the 250 kilometer trip, especially when compared with the later journey from Neapolis to Troas which took five days (Acts 20:6). It would only have been possible if a relatively strong south wind had been present to counteract the effect of the current flowing out of the Bosporus.[1] The nautical term used in Acts 16:11, "sailing out before the wind,"[2] tends to confirm this view. In the Aegean Sea the south wind brought winter rains and storms, continuing intermittently into the spring. It could be expected from March, when sailing opened in the Mediterranean, until June. In the later summer, when the northerly etesian ruled the Aegean, such a south

wind is and was practically unheard of.[3] In all probability Paul and his
party would have had to sail in the spring to make such good time on this
part of the sea.[4] This datum could be correlated with the arrival in Corinth later in the same expedition so as to make some deductions regarding
the length of Paul's stay in Philippi.

## PAUL'S STAY IN EPHESUS UNTIL PENTECOST

In 1 Cor. 16:8 Paul refers to his decision to remain in Ephesus until
Pentecost. Although the complicated question of whether he actually carried through with this travel plan must be dealt with in connection with
the total Corinthian correspondence, it is at least clear that this reference
provides a seasonal *terminus ad quem* for the writing of this verse.

The date of Pentecost falls seven weeks after Passover, which takes
place on the 15th of Nisan. J. Goudoever has shown that Acts and the
early Christian tradition in general followed the Zadokite dating system
whereby the first of the fifty days falls on the first Sunday after Passover.[5]
There are notorious difficulties in predicting how accurately ancient ob-
servers caught the first light of new moons,[6] so that discrepancies of a day
or so are entirely possible. But when one uses such data simply to provide
a *terminus ad quem*, such minor discrepancies will have no impact on the
chronology as a whole. The following table of dates between A.D. 52 and
60 is based on Plooij's calculations of the first of Nisan.[7] The selection of
the year 1 Cor. 16:8 was written depends on correlation with other data.

| Year | 1st of Nisan | 15th Nisan Passover | 15th Nisan Day of Week | 1st Sunday after Passover | Date of Pentecost |
|------|-------------|---------------------|------------------------|---------------------------|-------------------|
| 52 | March 21 | April 4 | Tuesday | April 9 | June 7 |
| 53 | April 9 | April 23 | Wednesday | April 27 | May 24 |
| 54 | March 29 | April 12 | Friday | April 14 | June 2 |
| 55 | March 18 | April 1 | Tuesday | April 6 | May 25 |
| 56 | April 5 | April 19 | Wednesday | April 23 | June 11 |
| 57 | March 25 | April 8 | Friday | April 10 | May 29 |
| 58 | March 14 | March 28 | Tuesday | April 2 | May 21 |
| 59 | March 4 | March 18 | Saturday | March 19 | May 7 |
| 60 | March 22 | April 5 | Saturday | April 6 | May 25 |

PAUL'S DEPARTURE FROM PHILIPPI

The date of Paul's departure from Philippi on the last Jerusalem trip (Acts 20:6ff.) has been reckoned by Ramsay[8] and Plooij[9] to be on Friday the 15th of April, 57. They reasoned that since Paul departed from Troas on a Monday (Acts 20:11) following a seven day visit (20:6), he must have arrived there on the previous Tuesday. Since the trip from Philippi had lasted five days, Paul must have departed on the previous Friday. Now this Friday followed immediately upon the close of the feast of Unleavened Bread (20:6). A study of astronomical tables showed that only in the years 54 and 57 did the day following the close of this feast fall on a Friday.

Oswald Gerhardt reached a different result when he applied the astronomical method to the premise that Paul's seven day visit in Troas did not count the day of departure, hence falling on the preceding Monday.[10] Then he reckoned the five day trip from Philippi without counting the day of arrival, which drives the departure date back to a Wednesday following the close of the feast. Given the fact that the Jewish custom of counting days always included portions of days as whole days, the problematic aspects of this reading of Acts 20:5–11 are visible in the following illustration:

| *Ramsay and Plooij:* | | *Gerhardt:* |
|---|---|---|
| | TUESDAY | End of Festival |
| | WEDNESDAY | Departure from Philippi |
| End of Festival | THURSDAY | Five |
| Departure from Philippi | FRIDAY | Day |
| Five | SATURDAY | Journey |
| Day | SUNDAY | |
| Journey | MONDAY | Arrival in Troas |
| Arrival in Troas | TUESDAY | Seven |
| Seven | WEDNESDAY | Day |
| Day Visit | THURSDAY | Visit |
| | FRIDAY | |
| | SATURDAY | |
| | SUNDAY | |
| Departure from Troas | MONDAY | Departure from Troas |

Unfortunately Gerhardt did not argue his reading of these verses in detail, depending entirely upon Theodor Zahn's commentary on the Book of Acts.[11] His conclusion that the Festival ended on Tuesday, the 28th of March, A.D. 58, seems therefore the less plausible of the two approaches.

Several objections to this entire effort have been raised. Haenchen suggested that there may have been several days between the end of the Festival of Unleavened Bread and the departure from Troas,[12] which would of course invalidate the astronomical calculations. The effectiveness of this criticism depends on the attitude one takes on the authenticity of the "we-source," which begins with 20:6. If this is truly travel diary material, would the person who noted that the trip to Troas lasted five days and the visit there seven days not be likely to report something like "three days after the feast" if such had been the time of departure? As noted above in Chapter I, the writer of the "we-source" seems to provide exact intervals whenever he can, of one day (28:13), three days (25:1; 28:11; 28:17), five days (24:1; 20:13), and so forth. George Ogg's objections share the same flaw, that the ship from Philippi's harbor of Neapolis may not have set sail the day they left Philippi, and that the famous evening sermon in Troas at the conclusion of Paul's stay there may have been on what we would call Saturday night rather than Sunday night.[13] On the latter point, Julian Morgenstern showed through an extensive analysis of the references to "next day" in Acts 4:3-5; 20:7-11; 10:3-23; and 23:15, 20, 23 that "the day was reckoned from sunrise to sunrise."[14] Finally Ogg argues that Paul's resolution to avoid Ephesus so as to arrive in Jerusalem by Pentecost (Acts 20:16) does not necessarily mean that Paul had left Philippi on schedule, because the resolution may have emerged as a result of subsequent delays. Even if this were plausible, it would not invalidate the astronomical reckoning.[15] In conclusion, although the historian would hesitate to base an entire chronology on this kind of astronomical calculation, no convincing objection has been raised to incorporating the alternative departure dates into the hypothesis if one of them happens to fit: April 19, A.D. 54, or April 15, 57. It is perhaps worth pointing out that the principal critics are committed to chronologies that would disallow both of these dates and the Gerhardt reckoning as well.[16]

## PAUL'S DEPARTURE FROM FAIR HAVENS

In Acts 27:9 there is a seasonal reference to the Day of Atonement fast which serves to indicate the approach of the stormy season when sailing is dangerous. W. P. Workman suggested that the second *kai* in this sentence implies that "even the fast had gone by," which means that some other recognizable date for hazardous navigation had passed just before it.[17] Arguing that the autumn equinox was the date in question,[18] Workman felt that only in the year 59 did the fast occur long enough after the equinox for the three and a half months of the storm and the Malta sojourn to bring the party down to the opening of sailing in February. This has been widely rejected as inconclusive, in part because Vegetius' reference to the 14th of September as the close of safe sailing may well have been assumed.[19] A discrepancy in the three and a half month sequence would still remain, since it was generally accepted that the sailing season did not open until the first week of March.[20] But the chronological pressure of the detailed account of the shipwreck and the Malta sojourn require the latest possible departure from Fair Havens, and the fact that the "fast" rather than the "Feast of Tabernacles" was mentioned indicates the conversation took place in the five day period between these two events in the Jewish calendar. The Feast of Tabernacles was the traditional end of the safe sailing season in the Jewish tradition.[21] It would surely have been referred to if it had already taken place at the time of the conversation between Paul and the centurion.[22] The following illustration shows the chronological implications of the details in the "we-source," beginning with the October 5 Atonement Day fast in A.D. 59 as compared with the September 16 date for Atonement in the preceding year.

| *A.D. 58:* | *A.D. 59:* | *Events in Acts 27:8–28:11:* |
|---|---|---|
| Sept. 16 | Oct. 5 | Day of Atonement |
| Sept. 19 | Oct. 8 | Point between Atonement and Feast of Tabernacles when conversation in 27:9–10 occurred |
| Sept. 26 | Oct. 15 | Estimated *terminus ad quem*[23] for departure with gentle south wind, Acts 27:13 |
| Sept. 29 | Oct. 18 | Three day period of attempting to cope with the storm, Acts 27:14–19 |
| Oct. 13 | Nov. 1 | End of fourteen days adrift in ship, Acts 27:27,33 |
| Oct. 14 | Nov. 2 | Ashore on Malta, Acts 27:39–44 |

| Oct. 17 | Nov. 5 | End of three days in Publius' home, Acts 28:7 |
| Jan. 17 | Feb. 5 | End of three months additional stay on Malta, Acts 28:11 |

Since there are some precedents for sailing in early February,[24] the chronology in A.D. 59 is possible, though one would not wish to vouch for the prudence of risking the spring storms after an experience such as they had undergone. The schedule in a year like A.D. 58 on the other hand is inconceivable. So Workman's choice of A.D. 59 as the most logical date for the departure retains some plausibility since that year has the latest Day of Atonement of any year from A.D. 55–62.

## THE TIME-SPANS IN GALATIANS 1–2

When Paul speaks of the three year and the fourteen year spans, what is his point of reference? Do both spans begin with the conversion, thus making the fourteen years a cumulative total or do the spans follow one another in consecutive order? This question has been debated for centuries,[25] and the fact that it was ever raised in the first place is an indication of the pressure within Pauline chronology. Scholars have had as much difficulty fitting the seventeen year time-span into the Lukan framework as they have in reconciling Galatians with Acts. The reason for reducing the seventeen years to fourteen, or even four,[26] has been to remove the compression between the Apostolic Conference and the conversion. This crucial issue will be taken up in Chapter V, but for the sake of impartial treatment of the exegetical problems, all thought of the resultant implications for Pauline chronology must be excluded.

The plain sense of the thrice repeated *epeita*/"then" in Galatians 1–2 is consecutive, not cumulative. The expression "then after three years" in 1:18 refers back to the "when" in v. 15. The "then I went" of v. 21 expresses in clear consecutive sequence what happened after the first Jerusalem journey. Finally the words "then after fourteen years" (2:1) specify the span of time since the previous Jerusalem journey mentioned in 1:18. That the fourteen years are measured from the first Jerusalem journey rather than from the conversion is clearly indicated by the wording, with "I went up again to Jerusalem" in 2:1 referring back to "I went up to Jerusalem" in 1:18. Not only does the "again" point back to the earlier reference to a Jerusalem visit, but the slightly varied parallel form of the statements brings the reader's attention at 2:1 automatically back to 1:18. Furthermore, as Lightfoot and Burton have argued, the use of *dia* in Gal. 2:1 as contrasted with *meta* in 1:18 expresses the nuance that Paul had not been in contact with the Jerusalem leaders through the entire fourteen year period.[27] The preposition *dia* in this context requires the translation "after" the completion of the fourteen year no-contact period, as Sieffert and Bauer have shown.[28] This would tend to eliminate the cumulative argument which places the Jerusalem trip three years after the beginning of the fourteen year span.[29]

A great deal of evidence could be adduced in substantiation of this conclusion. Bauer states plainly that *epeita* denotes "succession . . . chronological sequence";[30] Moulton–Milligan note that this word always expresses a procession of time;[31] Liddell–Scott define the word as expressing "mere sequence, without any notion of cause."[32] An analysis of Paul's frequent use of this word shows that he always employs it in a strictly consecutive sense. In 1 Thess. 4:17 it expresses the sequence of the parousia wherein the believers yet alive will follow after those already dead in Christ; in 1 Cor. 12:28 it is used in a numerical sequence, "first apostles, second prophets, third teachers, then workers of miracles, then healers . . ." The most notable example is 1 Corinthians 15 where it is used four times (counting textual variants) to depict the sequence of resurrection appearances (15:5, 6, 7, 7) and then twice more to denote the sequence of the eschatological events (15:23, 46).

There can scarcely be any doubt, therefore, that the fourteen year span in Gal. 2:1 follows consecutively after the three year span mentioned in 1:8. The only question that remains is whether these spans must be reckoned as seventeen full years or whether the so-called "ancient method of reckoning time" was in use here—whereby any fraction of a year was counted as a whole year.[33] Under this assumption, the fractional years at the beginning and at the end of the time-span could be counted as full years. This could bring the three year span down to a little over one year and the fourteen years down to something over twelve. One cannot avoid noting, however, that the proponents of this method of reckoning all seem to be under the pressure of time in their own chronologies. For example, since Ramsay places the Galatians 2 visit in 45 and Schwartz in 43, the necessity arises to reduce the seventeen years to thirteen or less. When one notes the inclination of other specialists in chronology—who are not under such pressure—to reckon the seventeen years out in full,[34] one is inclined to examine the universality of the "ancient method." The exceptions to this method make themselves immediately apparent. One discovers, for example, that the Jews reckoned a man's age and the length of a king's reign only on the basis of completed years.[35] It is also interesting to recall that Luke does not fit into the "ancient method," because he usually specifies the number of months rather than rounding off to a year. Furthermore, with the multiplicity of calendars in the first century A.D.—the Jewish calendar alone having the religious year starting on 1 Nisan and the civil year on 1 Tishri—it is more logical to assume that Paul used full years as Luke did when addressing a heterogeneous audience. How would the Galatians know whether Paul reckoned on the North Syrian method with the New Year in the fall or the South Syrian method with the New Year in the spring, or the Roman method with the New Year on January 1? Even the learned W. M. Ramsay found it impossible to answer this question.[36]

Even if Paul reckoned the spans on the partial year system, why wouldn't the three year designation just as easily represent two years and eleven months as one year and a month? If one were to use mathematical probabilities, the average would presumably be two and thirteen years respectively. But how can such probabilities be useful in making decisions about specific events? History, after all, is the arena of the unique rather than the average. The only safe assumption is that even if Paul did not designate full years, the partial system might have come very close to the full three and fourteen year spans. If a chronology does not proceed on this assumption, its starting point will appear arbitrary. Despite any difficulties that might arise in the final chronology, it must be assumed that Paul's time-spans add up to seventeen full calendric years.

## THE PROBLEM OF THE VISION
## "FOURTEEN YEARS AGO"

In 2 Cor. 12:2-4 Paul alludes to an ecstatic experience that occurred "fourteen years ago," in which he was transported "into Paradise" and "heard things that cannot be told." If this experience could be identified with some phase or event in Paul's ministry, that event could be dated fourteen years before the writing of 2 Corinthians 12. Several rather implausible suggestions have been made to integrate this datum into Pauline chronology. Bruston, Goguel, and Giet connected the vision with the one reported in Acts 22:17,[37] despite the fact that the content of the latter could be described publicly, while the former was inexpressible. The Acts 22:17 vision was reportedly a warning to leave Jerusalem and it had nothing to do with "Paradise." Knox and Buck-Taylor identified the vision with Paul's conversion on the road to Damascus,[38] again despite the fact that Paul is twice reported to have publicly described this experience (Acts 22:6-11; 26:12-18). Knox later recognized "that the description here (2 Cor. 12:2-4) does not fit well with other references to the conversion and therefore that the two intervals of fourteen years are probably a mere coincidence."[39] A third identification of the ecstatic experience with Paul's arrival in Antioch (Acts 11:25-26) was suggested by Zahn, Bachmann, Allo, and Gunther.[40] But there is no hint of an ecstatic experience in this account of Barnabas recruiting Paul for the Antioch ministry.

One must conclude that since there is no sure way to correlate the paradise vision with some other event in Paul's life, it is unusable for general chronological purposes. All one can conclude for the sake of Pauline biography is that the experience in question occurred fourteen years before the writing of 2 Corinthians 12.

THE TIME-SPANS IN ACTS

There are several references to seasons and time-spans in Acts that should be taken into consideration. Acts 20:3 refers to a three month visit in Corinth, which corresponds to the plan in 1 Cor. 16:6 to "winter" there. This corroboration tends to sustain the conclusion that such details in Acts, when not motivated directly by the salvation–history scheme, are relatively trustworthy historical data. It also indicates that the author is not in the habit of carelessly rounding off his fractions to years. It is consistent therefore that the Corinthian ministry was not a rounded off two years but a more specific year and six months (Acts 18:11). When the three months (Acts 19:8) and two years (Acts 19:10) of the Ephesian ministry are rounded off it is done ostensibly not by Luke but by Paul, in whose speech it occurs (Acts 20:31). One might add, parenthetically, that Luke actually gives no cumulative total for the Ephesian ministry. He simply specifies three months in the synagogue and two years of open preaching in the Hall of Tyrannus. Paul may well have stayed on in Ephesus some months after a crisis had curtailed a continuation of open proselytizing. The figure of three years which Luke has him specify may indicate a period cf approximately 36 months in Ephesus and its vicinity for the total ministry in Asia (Acts 20:18). The reconstructed sequence of the Corinthian correspondence indicates that Paul did in fact continue to focus his activities in the area of Ephesus for several months after the crisis and imprisonment that ended his public ministry there. It appears, at any rate, that the three year designation is more than a rounded off two and a quarter years. There is reason to assume, therefore, that the two years of Paul's imprisonments in Caesarea (Acts 24:27) and Rome (Acts 28:30), as well as the three months in Malta (Acts 28:11) are relatively full and precise designations. Since previous chronologies have so often been under a time pressure requiring the compression of these spans into shorter periods, it would be advisable to regard each as a full period and to find room for it as such.

MISCELLANEOUS SEASONAL DATA

When a detailed chronology is being reckoned out over a period of several decades, it is essential that seasonal data be taken into account. Each detail, though relatively insignificant in and by itself, assumes a larger importance as it fits into a connected itinerary. Merrill F. Unger has suggested one such detail in connection with the missionary expedition reported in Acts 13-14.[41] Since the prevailing winds in the spring and summer are westerly in this part of the Mediterranean, forcing travelers from Antioch to Cyprus to skirt the Cilician coast and come down to a northern port, it seems likely that the journey from Antioch to Salamis on the east coast of Cyprus was made at the very beginning of the sailing season before the westerlies began.[42] Although exceptional weather conditions may have occurred, it seems appropriate to assume a departure in early March.

There are several seasonal indications directly mentioned in Acts and the letters. Paul's reference to wintering in Corinth (1 Cor. 16:6) is quite clear, as is his statement in 1 Cor. 16:8 about remaining in Ephesus until Pentecost. Acts' reference to the Feast of Unleavened Bread (20:6), Pentecost (20:16), and the Atonement Day fast (27:9) may be accurate, although one must be suspicious of Luke's portrayal of Paul's eagerness to celebrate such festivals (cf. 20:16) and observances (cf. 18:18; 21:26). Of equal significance, however, are the seasonal contingencies that are not mentioned in the sources. For example, it is known that sea travel was generally closed from mid-November until March. It was considered dangerous from mid-September until the latter part of May.[43] Similarly, the Jewish tradition was that sailing was safe only from Pentecost till the Feast of Tabernacles.[44] The reasons for the relatively complete cessation of sea travel in the winter were not only the threat of storms but also the difficulties of navigating on short winter days and cloudy nights.[45]

Road travel was similarly curtailed in the winter. Vegetius states that it was closed from mid-November until mid-March just as sea travel

was.[46] The letters of Basil of Caesarea, for example, indicate that travel
for ordinary persons was suspended until Easter.[47] The ancients felt that
travel in mountainous areas was especially risky in the winter, and Ramsay notes in the case of the Taurus Mountains over which Paul traveled
that they are ". . . for the most part really dangerous to cross in winter,
owing to the deep snow obliterating the roads."[48] Although one cannot
rule out the possibility that Paul and his party might have taken advantage of unseasonably good travel conditions even in the winter, it is none-
theless a sound working assumption that they followed the customary
limits. If he "wintered" in Corinth, one can safely assume that he took the
normal precautions in other years as well.

As a result one must exclude the winter months for such sea journeys
as those from Seleucia to Cyprus (Acts 13:4), Cyprus to Perga (Acts
13:13), Attilia to Antioch (Acts 14:25–26), Antioch to Cyprus (Acts
15:39), Beroea to Athens (Acts 17:14), Corinth through Ephesus to Syria
(Acts 18:18–21), and Troas to Macedonia (2 Cor. 2:12–14). It is also
proper to assume that Paul would not start over the Taurus Mountains in
the late fall or winter during either the second or third missionary expeditions (Acts 15:41; 18:23).[49]

## THE TIMETABLE FROM JERUSALEM
## TO CORINTH

A crucial period for Pauline chronology lies between the traditional
date of the Apostolic Conference (Acts 15) and the arrival in Corinth
(Acts 18:1), datable on the basis of the Gallio inscription. This period
receives special attention because the seventeen year span preceding the
Apostolic Conference pushes it in one direction and the Gallio datum in
the other. In some chronologies these travels are compressed into the six
months between the summer and winter of A.D. 49. In other systems the
date of summer 48 for the Apostolic Conference allows an eighteen
month period.[50] On the suspicion that these travels may have taken even
longer,[51] a detailed itinerary will be worked out here. For reasons of
method, no external pressures and no chronological consequences will be
allowed to distort the schedule of these travels and missionary visits.

The journey to Corinth, according to the present consensus, began in
Jerusalem, led through Antioch and Cilicia to Derbe, Lystra, Iconium,
and Antioch on the main trade route toward Asia. Barred from entering
Asia, Paul turned north with the intent of entering Bithynia, passing
through the area of Phrygia and on into Galatia proper. Having estab-

lished churches in the North Galatian cities,[52] Paul is thwarted from entering Bithynia and thus departs from the main roads and travels across the
mountains on unknown paths to Troas from whence he goes by ship to
Philippi. He establishes churches in Philippi, Thessalonica, and Beroea
before traveling on to Athens, the last stop before arrival in Corinth in
the winter of A.D. 49–50. If this journey were made by the most direct
route, it would cover a land distance of an estimated 2722 kilometers and
a sea distance of 775 kilometers.[53] Assuming for the sake of argument that
Paul and his party could have maintained the pace of 30 kilometers per
day across the Anatolian highlands, a minimum of 90 days would be spent
on the land journey alone.[54] Considering possible detours and the mountainous terrain, a longer period of time would be more probable.

The length of stay in each town is of course more difficult to estimate,
but the fact that Paul later spent eighteen months establishing the church
in Corinth (Acts 18:11) and over two years in Ephesus (Acts 20:31), and
that he spent three months in revisiting Corinth (Acts 20:3), provides us
with a measure to work out estimates. Paul must have spent at least two
months in Antioch (Acts 15:30–39; Gal. 2:11ff.),[55] and probably several
months visiting the other churches in Syria and Cilicia (Acts 15:49) before
starting over the Taurus Mountains. Since he was working out the arrangements for the Jerusalem collection (Gal. 2:10; Acts 15:41; 16:4), he probably would have had to spend at least a month in each of the congregations at Lystra, Derbe, Iconium, and Pisidian Antioch. In several of these
cities Paul would have had to pause to exercise his trade to support the
next leg of the journey, since he was entering now into the independent
phase of his mission (cf. Acts 15:39–40; Phil. 4:15). The establishment of
several churches (cf. Gal. 1:1) in North Galatia along with the delays
caused by his illness there (Gal. 4:13ff.) probably took nine months to a
year; the establishment of a church at Troas (Acts 16:10ff.; 20:6–12)
would require several months; and the ministry in Philippi (Acts 16:12ff.)
probably took six months to a year. The deep bonds of affection between
Paul and the Philippians reflected in the letter lead one to prefer the
longer estimate. If the ministry at Thessalonica was cut short after three
or four months (1 Thess. 2:17), and if that in Beroea lasted two months,
and the fruitless ministry in Athens one month, then the entire journey
from Jerusalem to Corinth would have taken between three and four
years.[56]

In order to compress the Jerusalem–Corinth itinerary to a minimum
period approaching the traditional eighteen month duration, one would

have to reduce the visits to incredibly short spans. One would have to assume that Paul and his party traveled at a speed of 40 kilometers per day and that they never were hampered by ship connections or bad weather. The following table illustrates the problem.

| Travels and Visits: | Kilometers | Minimum Time[57] | Normal Time[58] |
|---|---|---|---|
| 1. Jerusalem to Antioch (Acts 15:30) | 600 k. | 15 days | 4 weeks |
| 2. Visit in Antioch (Acts 15:30–39); long enough for word to return to Jerusalem that Peter was eating with the gentiles and for a representative of James to arrive (Gal. 2:11ff.) | | 7 weeks | 4 months |
| 3. Antioch to Derbe (Acts 15:41–16:1) (Antioch, Alexandreia, Mopsuestia, Tarsus)[59] (Tarsus, Podandos, Herecleia-Cybistra, Kastabala, Barata, Derbe)[60] | 471 k. (238 k.) (233 k.) | 12 days | 3 weeks |
| 4. Visits to churches in Syria, Cilicia, and Derbe (Acts 15:41) | | 5 weeks | 10 weeks |
| 5. Derbe through Lystra to Iconium (Acts 16:1–5)[61] | 144 k. | 3 days | 4 days |
| 6. Visits in Lystra and Iconium (Acts 16:4–5) | | 2 weeks | 8 weeks |
| 7. From Iconium to Neapolis and Antioch in Pisidia (Acts 16:6 implies western movement toward Asia; Acts 15:41; 16:4; and Gal. 2:10 indicate Paul visited churches to organize the collection)[62] | 142 k. | 3 days | 4 days |
| 8. Visit in Antioch in Pisidia (Acts 16:4–5) | | 1 week | 4 weeks |
| 9. Pisidian Antioch to Ancyra (Acts 16:6–7; Gal. 1:2; 3:1); journey to north Galatia, far enough north | | | |

| *Travels and Visits:* | *Kilometers* | *Minimum Time*[57] | *Normal Time*[58] |
|---|---|---|---|
| to be "opposite of Mysia" and to be at the approach to Bithynia. (Antioch, Philomelium, Amorium, Pessimus, Germa, Ancyra)[63] | 312 k. | 8 days | 2 weeks |
| 10. Missionary Activity in North Galatia, probably in Pessimus, Germa, and Ancyra, including period of illness (Gal. 4:13ff.) | | 6 mo. | 1 year |
| 11. Ancyra to Troas, skirting Mysia (Acts 16:8) (Ancyra, Germa, Dorylaion, Cotiaion)[64] (Cotiaion, Aesani, Cadi, Ancyra Sidera, . . . on unknown road, Adramyttion, Assos, Troas)[65] | 771 k. (313 k.) (458 k.) | 20 days | 6 weeks |
| 12. Missionary Activity in Troas (Acts 16:10ff.; 20:6–12) | | 2 weeks | 8 weeks |
| 13. Troas to Philippi through Neopolis (Acts 16:11) by sea | 250 k. | 3 days | 3 days |
| 14. Missionary Activity in Philippi (Acts 16:12ff.) | | 3 mo. | 1 year |
| 15. Philippi to Thessalonica (Acts 17:1) | 140 k. | 4 days | 4 days |
| 16. Thessalonian Mission (Acts 17:1–9) | | 3 mo. | 4 mo. |
| 17. Thessalonica to Beroea (Acts 17:10) | 70 k. | 2 days | 2 days |
| 18. Beroean Ministry (Acts 17:10–14)[66] | | 2 mo. | 2 mo. |
| 19. Beroea to Athens (Acts 17:15–16) (By land to Pydna and from Piraeus to Athens) (By sea from Pydna to Piraeus) | 56 k. 450 k. | 10 days | 2 weeks |
| 20. Ministry in Athens (Acts 17:16–34) | | 2 weeks | 4 weeks |

| Travels and Visits: | Kilometers | Minimum Time[57] | Normal Time[58] |
|---|---|---|---|
| 21. Athens through Piraeus, by ship to Cenchraea, on to Corinth (Acts 18:1) | | | |
| By land: | 16 k. | | |
| By sea: | 75 k. | 3 days | 3 days |
| TOTALS | 3497 k. | 91 weeks | 201 weeks |
| (By Sea: | 775 k.) | | |
| (By Land: | 2722 k.) | (640 days) | (1409 days) |

The "normal" travel schedule from Jerusalem to Corinth, based on estimates that correlate with travels and missionary activity in the later, more accessible part of Paul's life, consumes more than twice as much time as the eighteen month period normally allotted by Pauline chronologies of the traditional type. Even the minimum schedule runs thirteen weeks over the traditional eighteen month period. The following reductions would be necessary to compress this journey into the traditional time–span:

—visits to the churches of Syria, Cilicia and Derbe, from a "normal" estimate of 10 weeks, to 3 weeks;

—mission establishing the churches in Galatia, from a "normal" estimate of 52 weeks, to 14 weeks;

—mission establishing the church in Troas, from a "normal" estimate of 8 weeks, to 1 week;

—mission establishing the church in Philippi, from a "normal" estimate of 52 weeks, to 9 weeks;

—mission in Athens from a "normal" estimate of 4 weeks to 1 week.

The result of such compression would be a picture of Paul and his missionary activity that differs drastically from that reflected in his letters and the later portions of Acts. It would be the picture of a man with the constitution of a marathon runner, capable of averaging more than 40 kilometers per day (cf. 2 Cor. 12:5–10) who is never detained by shipwrecks, blizzards, floods, mountains, robbers, or imprisonment (cf. 2 Cor. 11:23–29); a man with sufficient means to finance himself and his associates without working along the way (cf. 1 Thess. 2:9; 2 Thess. 3:7–8; Phil. 4:14–16); one who succeeds in establishing churches with miraculous speed without taking time for doctrinal or ethical instruction (cf. 1 Thess. 4:1–2; 5:1–2; 1 Cor. 15:1–11; 11:2, 23–26, etc.); a man whose

previously established congregations lead such an unproblematic existence that they need not be revisited for any length of time; in short a man
more divine than human. Compressing the journey from Jerusalem to
Corinth into an eighteen month period, though theoretically possible,
leaves no time for the indecisiveness reflected in the canceled plans to
enter Asia (Acts 16:7), and then Bithynia (Acts 16:7), which finally
issued in the unexpected vision to cross to Macedonia (Acts 16:9). While
theoretically possible, it is highly improbable. And as for the compression
into six months, it is simply impossible. The safe assumption for the historian is that this journey moved at the pace of Paul's later missionary
travels, thus consuming between three and four years.

# CHAPTER IV

# TESTING PREVIOUS CHRONOLOGIES AGAINST THE EVIDENCE

An effective evaluation of previous hypotheses requires the application of clearly stated critical principles. The absence of such critical tools invites the play of subjective judgment, or it may reduce a history of research to a vast and incomprehensible chronicle. In an experimental study the most appropriate critical tools are the objective data themselves. The canon proposed here is the degree to which each hypothesis succeeds in utilizing the ascertainable dates and time–spans. The systematic application of this canon allows one to view the bewildering variety of chronological hypotheses as experiments whose usefulness is both positive and negative. The relative failures eliminate certain experimental options and the relative successes point the way toward a potential solution. Although the relentless application of such a canon may seem to evoke harsh judgments upon the work of many great scholars, a fundamental respect and appreciation is implicit, for without both negative and positive contributions no meaningful progress could be made. Each of these hypotheses, reflecting the integrity and ingenuity of trained minds from differing cultures and times, can be utilized in an experimental manner as a kind of roadmark on the way toward the solution of the problem of Pauline chronology.

The intensive chronological discussion before the turn of the last century hinged on the problem of relating the journeys in Acts with the data in the letters. It appeared that every conceivable combination had already been tried and found lacking. Thus the famous J. B. Lightfoot concluded in his lectures of the 1870s: "On the subject of the chronology of St. Paul's life originality is out of the question. Unless new documents are discovered to throw fresh light upon the period, little or nothing can be added to our present stock of knowledge."[1] The debate during this period largely lacked the discipline imposed by the later discovery of such pivotal dates

as the Gallio proconsulship. As a result, the problem of conflicts between
the data in Acts and the letters was not generally recognized. A glance at
Adolf von Harnack's chronology affords an insight into the rather hap-
hazard state of the debate at the end of the century. At the same time,
his work serves to introduce the first basic type of chronology that attempts to reconcile the evidence in the letters with the Lukan framework
of five Jerusalem journeys.

## CHRONOLOGIES ON THE LUKAN FRAMEWORK

### A. Acts 15 Identical with Galatians 2

Harnack follows the majority opinion among NT scholars of his time
that the so-called "Apostolic Conference" described in Acts 15 is to be
identified with the meeting described in Gal. 2:1–10.[2] When he moves
beyond this apparently solid start, the confusion is bewildering. He begins
with a mistaken dating of the Festus appointment in A.D. 56 that forces
Paul's last visit in Jerusalem back to 54. Although this results in moving
the arrival in Corinth back to the fall of 48, thus excluding any correlation with the Gallio data, he must still compress the fourth Jerusalem
journey into a matter of weeks. With the Apostolic Conference in 47, the
conversion is pushed back to 30, thus eliminating the Aretas datum. Although the resultant chronology suffers from pressure on both ends of
Paul's life, Harnack betrays not the slightest awareness of the problem
when he concludes: "So far as my knowledge extends, there is not a
single valid objection against any aspect of this chronology."[3] He must
have rued the day he made this claim, because in 1912 he corrected some
of the obvious mistakes by moving the conversion to 31, the Apostolic
Council to 48, and the arrival in Corinth to 49, on the basis of the Gallio
inscription and the Claudius edict.[4]

Gustav Hoennicke, in contrast to Harnack, was so impressed with the
difficulty of reconciling the data that he left virtually every question
open.[5] The conversion was sometime between 33–35, the first Jerusalem
journey between 36–38, and the Apostolic Conference between 50–52. But
placing the first Jerusalem trip this late in order to fit the Aretas datum
forced him to disregard the best information available in his own day
concerning the Gallio proconsulship, thus pushing it back to 53–54. Even
this adjustment of two years beyond the date later provided by the
Delphi inscription necessitated reducing the timetable from Jerusalem to
Corinth to less than a year. No matter how open the questions are left,
the dilemmas remain. Yet there is an impressive candor in setting time-

spans, in effect, for each major event in Paul's chronology: 59–61 for Festus' accession; 45–46 for the famine collection; 37–41 for Aretas' control of Damascus. But it is clear that a major cause for Hoennicke's inability to draw precise conclusions is his uncritical attitude toward Acts. In accepting its data as perfectly historical, he cannot eliminate the resultant conflicts with the letters and thus settles nothing.

A suitable starting point among chronologies written in English would be the influential work by Conybeare and Howson.[6] They use the Aretas datum and place the escape from Damascus in 38 with the conversion reckoned on the "ancient Judaic method" in 36. Then after Paul visits Jerusalem at the time of the famine in 45, he returns for the Apostolic Conference in 50. This assumes that the fourteen year designation in Galatians implied a few days over twelve years. Even with this compression Paul does not arrive in Corinth until six months after Gallio is known to have left. This results in compression of the period between the Corinthian and the Ephesian ministries. The trip from Corinth through Ephesus and Antioch to Jerusalem and back through all the congregations in Asia Minor is thereby forced into the incredibly short period from spring till fall in A.D. 54. Paul then travels in 58 to Jerusalem for the last time, is sent on to Rome in 60, released in 63, and finally executed in 68. Disregarding this rather fanciful late death of Paul's, one should note the impossibility of reconciling the Aretas date with the correct arrival in Corinth; even the most intense concern for historical accuracy is quite inadequate to reconcile these data with the Lukan framework.

C. H. Turner's chronology, which has become a prototype for many others, places the Apostolic Council at Pentecost 49 and the arrival in Corinth the following year.[7] This compression of the 3–4 year itinerary from Jerusalem to Corinth into one year is bought at the price of having Paul start over the Taurus Mountains in September and travel throughout the winter. Since the visitation of the various churches is reckoned to have taken at least seven months, the trip over Galatia—including Paul's period of sickness and indecision and the founding of the North Galatian churches—is compressed into a single month. The founding of the churches in Philippi, Thessalonica, Beroea, and the visit to Athens must therefore be compressed into the summer and early fall of 50. Then by placing Paul's arrest in Jerusalem in 56, only around four years remain from the departure from Corinth for the extensive activities reflected in the letters and Acts. But it is in the early period of Paul's chronology that Turner's commitment to the Lukan framework creates the most serious difficulties. To accept the Aretas date of the first Jerusalem journey in 38, the conversion has to be placed in 35, resulting in a reduction of the seventeen year span to fourteen years so as to reach the date of 49 for the Apostolic Conference. Turner's chronology retains its value because it reveals the dilemmas so clearly by reckoning out the travels and visits in detail.

A French chronologist who identifies Acts 15 with Galatians 2 is Henri Leclercq.[8] His work features an intensive investigation of the probable routes of the journeys and the use of archeological and historical data in ascertaining crucial dates. He places the conversion in 36 to make the first Jerusalem journey fit in with the escape from Aretas in 38 or 39. But as a result he must condense the fourteen year time-span to less than twelve in order to accommodate the Apostolic Conference in 49. Then he is forced to compress the timetable from Jerusalem to Corinth to less than eighteen months in order to have Paul arrive in the winter of 50–51 so as to correlate with the Gallio proconsulship. When Paul returns to Jerusalem after the Corinthian ministry, Leclercq pictures a very hurried itinerary, even having Paul start over the Taurus Mountains en route to Ephesus in the improbable season of the late fall. His chronology is completely in step with the evidence at the end of Paul's ministry, however, in placing the final departure from Philippi in 57 and the hearing before Festus in 59.

A typical presentation of the Acts 15 = Galatians 2 chronology may be found in Erich Fascher's encyclopedia article.[9] On the basis of the Gallio inscription he sets Paul's arrival in Corinth at the beginning of 50 which forces him to compress the extensive journey from Jerusalem into the eighteen month period before that, placing the Apostolic Conference in 48. He allows a full seventeen years prior to 48 for the conversion in 31, thus eliminating any correlation with the Aretas date. This admirable inclusion of the full seventeen year span also precluded acceptance of the more probable date for the crucifixion in 33; even the use of the alternate date of the crucifixion in 30 provides too short a span for the utilization of the eighteen month tradition of resurrection appearances or for churches to have been founded in points as distant as Damascus before Paul was converted. Fascher places Paul's arrest in Jerusalem on Pentecost 58 and the appearance before Festus in July, 60, which eliminates the use of the astronomical calculation of the departure from Philippi in 57 and the late departure from Fair Havens in 59. Despite these difficulties it is interesting to note that he refrains from discussing the problem of the conflicts between Luke and the Pauline letters. The chronology therefore contains the same internal problems and pressures as were visible in works fifty years earlier.

Even scholars who take a critical attitude toward Luke often resort in questions of chronology to the Lukan framework. In doing so they inevitably run into trouble. Ernst Haenchen, who criticizes even John Knox for ascribing too high a degree of historical credibility to Acts,[10] retains the Lukan outline except for the elimination of the Acts 11 collection journey to Jerusalem. The result is that with the conversion in 35 and the Apostolic Conference in 48 he must disallow Paul's statement regarding the seventeen year span. The Gallio date is used to place Paul's arrival in Corinth in the winter of 49–50. Then because he sets the Festus appointment in 55, Haenchen must assume Paul was taken to Rome in that same year. This involves a rejection of the two year Caesarean imprisonment and a compression of the activities of the third missionary period into the three short years after Paul's last trip west from Antioch. It also eliminates any correlation with the probable *terminus a quo* for the Egyptian rebel, the departure from Philippi in 57, the departure from Fair Havens in 59, and the *terminus a quo* for the beheading in 62. By retaining the theologically motivated Lukan framework of Jerusalem journeys he is forced into a rejection of dates and time–spans that have a much higher claim to historical validity. These problematic points in Haenchen's chronology are obscured by the lack of precise details in reckoning travels and time–spans. This is doubtless motivated by a skeptical attitude toward the Lukan data, but it presents serious barriers to an experimental approach which seeks to evaluate through replication.

Dieter Georgi's detailed reconstruction of the period from the Apostolic Conference until the delivering of the Jerusalem collection leads to several corrections of the Haenchen chronology.[11] Concurring with the dating of the conversion in 35, the Apostolic Council in 48, and the arrival in Corinth in the winter of 49–50, he breaks with Haenchen in allowing two and a half years for the Ephesian ministry and half a year for the travels from Ephesus to Macedonia. This results in a departure for Jerusalem around Pentecost 56. By placing the transfer of power from Felix to Festus in 58, the two year Caesarean imprisonment can be accommodated. Elements of compression still remain, however, because there would be no room in this later period for Paul's ministry "as far around as Illyricum" (Rom. 15:19), or for a second imprisonment in Asia during which Philemon apparently was written. The period between the Apostolic Conference and the arrival in Corinth is likewise compressed into the unlikely period of eighteen months and the seventeen year span between conversion and Apostolic Conference is reduced to Haenchen's thirteen year span. But Georgi's attempt to reconstruct the travels and communications concerning the Jerusalem collection from evidence in the Pauline letters makes this a valuable contribution to the chronological debate.

The chronology worked out by Cambier does a more adequate job of accommodating the seventeen year span by placing the conversion in 32–33 and the Apostolic Conference in 49.[12] But the retention of the Lukan framework which forces these dates into the period before Paul's arrival in Corinth thereby results in eliminating correlation with the Aretas datum. And the dating of the Conference in 49 results in pressure to get Paul to Corinth on time. Even by postponing the encounter with Gallio to the last possible moment, to the summer of 52, Cambier must compress the journey from Antioch to Corinth into the extremely short time between the autumn of 49 to the autumn of 50. In the English language version of this chronology the compression is slightly relieved by moving back the arrival in Corinth from the autumn to the winter of 50.[13] Even this is insufficient to provide time for an itinerary that would normally take three to four years. In contrast to the speed of this second missionary expedition, Cambier allows five full years for the third phase. This brings Paul to Jerusalem for an arrest in 58 that is probably a year too late. Since he favors the theory of a final period of missionary activity in Spain before an execution in 67, the end of Paul's life presumably was marked by relative leisure when compared to the frantic travels and activities between the Apostolic Conference and the departure from Corinth.

George Ogg[14] has produced the most valuable current presentation of the Lukan oriented chronology that identifies Galatians 2 with Acts 15. He manifests a judicious analysis of the ascertainable dates, a detailed reckoning of travel routes, and a healthy skepticism on such questions as the post–Roman ministry of Paul to Spain. Ogg reaches conclusions close to those of the present study in placing Aretas' control of Damascus between 37–40, the Claudius edict in the period from Jan. 25, 49, to Jan. 24, 59, and the Gallio proconsulship from May, 51, to May, 52. He argues for Festus' arrival in 61, later than most researchers would place it, a decision that accords with Ogg's elimination of the April 15, 57, departure from Philippi and the October, 59, departure from Fair Havens.

The inexorable pressures of a compromise chronology lead Ogg to compress the timetable from Jerusalem to Corinth on the second missionary journey into about eighteen months,[15] far too short to be credible. An even more serious difficulty is the compression of the seventeen year span mentioned in Galatians to the period between a conversion in 35 and the Apostolic Conference in 48. A tendency to downplay evidence in Paul's letters to accommodate contradictions with the Book of Acts is also visible in the weakly argued admission of a famine–relief mission between the two visits Paul described in Galatians 1–2. That "... it is the two visits to Jerusalem (i.e., Acquaintance and Conference Visits) which he [i.e., Paul] singles out that at the moment count with him and are, first the one and then the other, all his concern, and that the interval between them, with any visit to Jerusalem (i.e., the Famine Visit) ... is wholly out of his sight,"[16] does not correlate well with Paul's solemn statement in Gal. 1:18–24 that his relations with Jerusalem before the Apostolic Conference were limited to a single visit of fifteen days and that otherwise he "was still not known by sight to the churches of Christ in Judea." On most issues, however, Ogg provides a balanced sifting of the evidence that gives his study a viability far surpassing that of the compromise chronology itself. (For a listing of additional chronologies of this type, see note 17.)

## B. Acts 11 Identical with Galatians 2

As scholars after 1900 became increasingly conscious of the conflicts between Acts and the Pauline epistles, attention began to be devoted to the famine–relief mission. Its placement in Acts 11 seemed to contradict Paul's account in Galatians 1–2 of having made only two Jerusalem journeys up to and including the Apostolic Conference. Literary critics began to study this problem to discover reasons for the anomaly.

One of the first solutions to be offered was that of Eduard Schwartz which suggested that Acts 11 and 15 were a doublet of the same Jerusalem journey occurring during the famine of the early forties.[18] Schwartz placed the conference in the winter of 43–44 in order to precede the persecution by Agrippa's decree which supposedly banned Peter and others from Jerusalem. This necessitated reducing the seventeen year span to thirteen years to place the conversion in 30–31. This in turn pushed the date of the crucifixion back to 28–29, a measure whose improbability was increased by Schwartz's exclusion of the tradition of Paul's persecuting the church prior to his conversion because the intervening period was too short. That Paul's persecution of early Christianity was a Lukan invention seems implausible in light of direct references to this effect in Gal. 1:13,

23 and Phil. 3:6. The extremely early dating of the conversion also ignored
the Aretas datum. The conclusion of the chronology resulted in equal
violence to the ascertainable dates and time–spans because Schwartz
placed Felix's dismissal in the spring of 55. To avoid having Paul arrive
two years earlier than this for the arrest in Jerusalem, the two year span
in Acts 24:27 was connected with Felix's term rather than with Paul's
imprisonment, an incredible connection justified by "a healthy feeling for
language."[19] Schwartz made no attempt to fill in the details between 43
and 55, but it is clear that the Gallio datum would be impossible to reconcile with so early a conclusion to Paul's ministry.

Eduard Meyer attempted to improve upon the Schwartz hypothesis by
reckoning out the length of travels and time-spans.[20] Placing Paul's arrival
in Corinth in 50 on the basis of the Gallio inscription, he properly places
the beginning of the second missionary journey three years earlier. But
then the identification of the Apostolic Conference with Acts 11 results
in dating the conference in 43, before Agrippa's persecution of the church.
This forces Meyer to reduce the seventeen year span to fifteen in order
to set the conversion in 28. This requires that the crucifixion be pushed
back to 27 and that the Aretas datum be overlooked. On the other end
of the chronology, Meyer makes a rather unusual attempt to provide time
for everything. This leads him to postpone Paul's arrival in Jerusalem to
59 and his appearance before Festus to 61, thus eliminating any correlation with the astronomical reckoning of the departure from Philippi or
from Fair Havens. If one is conscientious enough to acknowledge the
weight of the travel data as Meyer does, even the experimental combination of Galatians 2 with Acts 11 cannot prevent the Lukan oriented chronology from disintegrating.

Some of those who identify Acts 11 with Galatians 2 are much less
critical than Schwartz of the Lukan outline, but this simply shifts the
pressure to other areas of the chronology. This may be seen in William
M. Ramsay's studies which carefully calculate the miles traveled and the
towns visited.[21] By placing the Galatians 2 visit in 45, which is actually
rather early for the famine reported in Acts 11, he finds it necessary to
reduce the seventeen year span to thirteen in order to place Paul's
conversion in 32, safely after the date of the crucifixion. This in turn
forces him to disregard the date of Paul's escape from Aretas. Then instead of reducing the number of Jerusalem journeys as Schwartz did,
Ramsay struggles to find room for three additional journeys after the
Apostolic Conference described in Galatians 2. The second Apostolic Con-

ference, reported in Acts 15, is placed in early 50 which necessitates a compression of the journey to Corinth into a period of eighteen months. Even this does not suffice because it forces one to assume that Paul remained in Corinth a full seven months after the last possible date for the Gallio hearing. The fourth visit to Jerusalem must then be turned into a flying trip of several months because Ramsay quite properly must place the final trip to Jerusalem in 57. There is no room in his chronology for the several Asian imprisonments, not to speak of the ministry as far west as Illyricum. Thus the efforts of one of the most learned geographers and historians ever to deal with this problem were not sufficient to fit the valid historical details into the framework Luke provides.

A valuable contribution to the chronological debate was worked out by Daniel Plooij.[22] He surveyed the previous discussion with a judicious eye and made a number of important observations and advances. Yet his reliance on the Lukan framework of Jerusalem journeys produced the typical pressures upon the ascertainable dates. By identifying the collection trip of Acts 11 with the Jerusalem visit of Galatians 2 in the winter of 45–46, he was forced to squeeze the first Jerusalem journey into the period thirteen years earlier and the conversion into the scant two years before that. Even this reduction of the seventeen year period to around fifteen years resulted in an all too early date of 30 for the conversion and forced him to reduce the relevance of the Aretas datum to a mere *terminus ad quem* of 40 for Paul's escape from Damascus. The retention of a second Apostolic Conference as reported in Acts 15 in the spring of 48 produces an anomaly of two identical meetings within a two year period, and the need to have Paul arrive in Corinth early in 50 compresses a journey which would normally have taken three or four years into twenty months. Since Plooij develops a conclusive case for Paul's departure from Philippi in 57, his Jerusalem arrest in the same year, and his journey to Rome in 59, the period from 50 to 57 is very compressed, leaving no time for the several trips to Corinth, the imprisonments in Asia, or the mission west to Illyricum.

A similarly valuable study of the ascertainable dates is Kirsopp Lake's "The Chronology of Acts."[23] After setting Paul's arrival in Corinth in late 49 or early 50, he allows adequate time for the extensive missionary activity and the travels from Jerusalem to Corinth by placing the Apostolic Conference in 46. But in identifying the conference with the famine visit and placing it this early, he is forced to pare down the seventeen year span to fit in the conversion in 32. In the process he eliminates the use of the Aretas date. Then in contrast to Plooij he places the arrest in Jerusalem in 55. This means that within the three short years between Paul's visit to Antioch in the winter of 51–52 and his stay in Corinth in the winter of 54–55, Lake must compress the revisitation of the churches of Asia Minor, the two and a quarter year ministry in Ephesus, the trips to Corinth, and the several imprisonments reflected in the Corinthian correspondence. Despite the outstanding example he provides in ascertaining some of the dates and time-spans, the problems in reconciling the data with the Lukan framework are insurmountable.

The most extensive statement of the Acts 11 = Galatians 2 chronology in English was written by John Gunther. He begins with an emphasis on the priority of the Pauline letters over the Book of Acts which would have pleased Eduard Schwartz: ". . . the most inherently trustworthy source of a chronology of Paul's earliest Christian years is his own account in Galatians 1–2."[24] An unwillingness to follow through with this priority surfaces in Gunther's reduction of the seventeen year span of Galatians to something between twelve and a half and thirteen and three quarters years. His reasoning is as follows: "If Paul cited numbers with the intent of demonstrating his independence, then both for clarity and emphasis he would refer to 'three' and 'fourteen' years after his call; for a mention of fourteen years with this meaning is rhetorically more emphatic than would be a reference to 'eleven' years . . ."[25] He supplies no grammatical evidence for the strained reading of the successive use of *epeita* and dismisses the evidence about Aretas' control of Damascus which derives from 2 Cor. 11:32, again violating his premise.[26] On the basis of the eighteen month period mentioned in the Ascension of Isaiah, Gunther dates the conversion in September, 31, and the second Jerusalem visit in 44–45. Since this is obviously too early for the Apostolic Conference in Acts 15, he identifies it as the "famine visit," thus contradicting Paul's description of the visit in Gal. 2:1–10 where there is not a hint about having brought famine relief.

Despite claims to the contrary Gunther is bound to the Lukan framework of five Jerusalem journeys throughout his chronology. The consequence is that the chronology suffers the usual time pressure in dating the Apostolic Conference proper in 48–49, which leaves only eighteen months for the extensive journey from Jerusalem to Corinth. The departure from Philippi is properly set in the spring of 57 and the hearing before Festus in 59, but the necessity to include the fourth Jerusalem journey in the period before 57 eliminates the possibility of including a ministry as far west as Illyricum mentioned in Rom. 15:19. Then on the assumption of Pauline authorship of the Pastoral Epistles and the questionable traditions about a Spanish mission, Gunther dates the writing of the former from Rome in 60–61 and places the latter in 62–64. Despite this problematic conclusion, Gunther's book provides a wide–ranging discussion of the scholarly literature, a solid discussion of textual critical problems such as Romans 16, and an innovative attempt to date the Epistle to the Hebrews as a product of a Pauline associate. But the lapses in applying the principle of the priority of the Pauline letters doom an otherwise impressive piece of work.

In studies strongly reminiscent of Eduard Schwartz's approach, S. Dockx uses literary critical arguments to excise two of the Jerusalem journeys mentioned in Acts.[27] By assigning 13:1–15:3 to a later insertion, the reference to coming to Jerusalem in 15:4 follows immediately after 12:25 on which Dockx prefers the variant "and Saul and Barnabas returned *to* Jerusalem . . ." By a strained interpretation of Acts 11:30 as a reference to the gathering rather than the delivering of the collection, Dockx consolidates the two reports into a single visit taking place after the death of Agrippa and prior to the commencement of the mission west to Corinth. This fusion of the famine relief trip and the Apostolic Conference eliminates the contradiction between Galatians 2 and Acts in the number of Jerusalem journeys prior to the Conference, but it does not solve the problem of time compression. The Apostolic Conference is placed in the late spring of 48, which results in a conversion date a little more than thirteen years earlier. This reduction of the seventeen year span allows Dockx to take account of the escape from Aretas in the summer of 37. The long itinerary from Jerusalem to Corinth is then compressed into the short period from the spring to November, 49. While this fusion of two Jerusalem journeys contributes nothing to the solution of the problem of time compression in the early part of Paul's ministry, the elimination of the Acts 18:22–23 Jerusalem journey relieves the pressure to some degree in the later period. This is more than offset, however, by Dockx's choice of July 1, 55 for Festus' arrival in Jerusalem. Even the improbable application of the "two years" in Acts 24:27 to Felix's total tenure rather than to Paul's period of imprisonment in Caesarea does not leave time for the Asian imprisonments or the mission west to Illyricum.[28] All the other dates and time–spans at the end of Paul's life are eliminated by the early termination of Paul's career after 55.

Alfred Suhl provides a sophisticated discussion of the chronological details visible in the letters, granting them precedence over the Book of Acts whose value is approached "heuristically."[29] The correlation between the letters and Acts follows the format of the Schwartz hypothesis, however, which creates some unavoidable distortions. Placing the Apostolic Conference in the winter of 43–44 produces compression even when Suhl reduces the seventeen year period from conference and conversion to fourteen years. It leads him to place the conversion in 30, much too close to the crucifixion in April of that year to be credible. And it leads to a violation of his natural *terminus ad quem* of spring, 43, for the Apostolic Conference because Acts 12:1–3 makes clear that the persecution occurred around Passover time. The method implicit in Suhl's study surfaces here, for he accepts Acts' information about Agrippa's persecution but dismisses the detail concerning the "days of unleavened bread."[30] Without developing an objective literary theory concerning the sources used in Acts, the method employed here is simply to accept details that fit the chronological necessity and reject those that do not. Suhl's acceptance of the Schwartz theory leads to an even more egregious violation of his usual respect for details in Paul's letters by concluding that the Aretas datum contributes nothing to chronology.[31] Having correctly assumed that Paul was a resident of Damascus prior to his persecution of Christians there, and that he did not return to Damascus after the first Jerusalem visit reported in Gal. 1:18–21,[32] it should be obvious that Paul's escape from the ethnarch of Aretas must precede this Jerusalem visit which Suhl dates three years after the conversion, i.e., A.D. 33. As noted in Chapter II, this is four full years before the earliest moment Aretas could have controlled Damascus. Suhl's suggestion that Aretas' patrols guarded the walls from the outside, presumably provoking Paul to drop over in a basket into their hands to escape them, has a preposterous logic that was similarly noted in Chapter II above.

There are several other difficulties in this, the most expert presentation of the hypothesis that Acts 11 = Galatians 2. Suhl places the missionary activity in Acts 13–14 after the Apostolic Conference and then sets the conflict with Peter at Antioch in the winter of 47–48. That four years intervened between Gal. 2:10 and 11 seems strange enough, but this results in Suhl's falling into the time compression trap in the itinerary between Antioch and Corinth, pressing several years' travel and missionizing into less than 18 months. Thus the Galatian churches were all founded in the winter of 48–49, the Philippian church in an incredible period of weeks, while the Thessalonian mission lasted the entire summer of 49. For the apparently successful missions in Troas and Beroea there remains no time at all as Paul strikes off in the fall of 49 to Illyricum.[33] The end of Paul's life is similarly constricted by Suhl's acceptance of an April, 55, departure with the offering to Jerusalem. This was calculated on the assumption that the offering aimed at relief during the sabbath year of 54–55, which is problematic because the most recent evidence indicates the sabbatical year was a year later.[34] Suhl correlates this with an eccentric calculation of the departure from Philippi that overlooks the solid calendric studies by Plooij and Goldstine.[35] The results of this early conclusion of Paul's mission are a reduction of the 27 month Ephesian ministry to less than two years, a compression of the entire Corinthian correspondence into an eight or nine month period in 54, and a conflation of the imprisonment reflected in Philemon, with its announced travel plan to visit Colossia, with the imprisonment implicit in Philippians, with its travel plan to visit Macedonia. Finally, by attaching the "two years" in Acts 24:27 to the tenure of Felix rather than to its more natural reference to the length of Paul's imprisonment, he brings Paul to the shipwrecked journey to Rome in 55–56, far too early to be coordinated with the date frames at the end of Paul's life. But the value of Suhl's study is not eliminated by these discrepancies, all of which are caused by the distorting pressures of the Schwartz hypothesis. This study remains a model of detailed historical reconstruction of the travel details and implications in the Pauline letters. Its insistence on the priority of evidence in the letters over that in Acts, though inconsistently carried through, provides a bridge to the "Epistle Oriented Chronologies." (For a listing of additional chronologies of the Acts 11 = Galatians 2 type, see note 36.)

EPISTLE ORIENTED CHRONOLOGIES

The second major type of chronology is based primarily on evidence within the Pauline epistles. Representatives of this type tend to be skeptical of the authenticity of Luke's chronological framework and, to a lesser degree, of the chronological details he provides. Convinced of the priority of evidence within Paul's letters, they have developed several approaches to the construction of the chronology.

*A. Developmental Schemes*

Donald W. Riddle relied entirely on evidence within the letters to construct a rough outline of Paul's life.[37] The crisis of the Apostolic Conference mentioned in Galatians 2 is used as the dividing point between the early letters (Thessalonians, 1 Corinthians, Colossians, Philemon, and a portion of Philippians) which contain no reference to the Judaizer problem and the later letters (2 Corinthians 10–13, Galatians and Phil. 3:2–16) which reflect the problem directly. Romans and 2 Corinthians 1–9 are assigned to the period after the Judaizer crisis had subsided. This scheme is combined with the equation of the fourteen year period in Galatians 2 with the vision "fourteen years ago" mentioned in 2 Cor. 12:2. Although Riddle admitted that the construction of a precise chronology on this basis "is impossible,"[38] it is clear that the arbitrary coordination of the fourteen year periods would raise insuperable barriers to a workable chronology. It is now clear to scholars that 2 Corinthians 10–13 does not deal with the Judaizer problem at all,[39] and no one accepts the curious idea that Colossians and Philemon belong to the early phase of Paul's ministry. The value of Riddle's work is thus limited to its sound argument for the methodical priority of the Pauline letters over Acts.

John C. Hurd, Jr. has offered an invaluable compilation of chronological hypotheses,[40] including those based on developmental schemes such as Riddle's.[41] Hurd suggests a synthesis of various developmental theories, using the majority–as–correct principle to produce the following outline of Paul's life and letters:[42] a) Jerusalem Visit ("acquaintance"); b) 1 and 2 Thessalonians; c) Previous Letter to Corinth (including 2 Cor. 6:14–7:1); d) Jerusalem Visit ("conference"; collection begins); e) 1 Corinthians; f) Philippians; g) 2 Corinthians 1–9; h) Galatians; i) Romans; j) (2 Corinthians 10–13) [parenthesis indicates the placement of this material cannot be settled by clear majority]; k) Jerusalem Visit (collection delivered; arrest); l) Colossians and Philemon; m) Ephesians—if genuine. Dates are not assigned to this outline, but the dilemmas are nevertheless obvious. Why is Galatians so far away from the conference it reports as recent history, while 1 and 2 Corinthians and Philippians immediately follow the conference without a single direct reference to it? A more revealing problem is that the use of the majority rule causes Hurd to place the "previous letter" before the conference, whereas he had taken pains in *The Origin of I Corinthians* to show why it should have immediately followed the conference.[43] The precariousness of deciding historical questions by majority rule is perfectly illustrated.

The most elaborate effort to base a chronology on a developmental scheme was worked out by Charles Buck and Greer Taylor.[44] They set about in systematic fashion to establish the sequence of the letters before taking up the question of the correlation with Acts. First they establish a normative basis of 1 Corinthians, 2 Corinthians 1–9 and Romans written in sequence because of references to the collection. They then make comparisons within this group of letters, suggesting advances in theology as the basis for dating other letters. 1 Thessalonians is placed early because its intense eschatological expectation is felt to be more primitive than 1 Corinthians. Comparisons in eschatology, law, and Christology are then argued to place Philippians between 1 Corinthians and 2 Corinthians 1–9. They overlook Phil. 4:5 "The Lord is at hand" in this discussion, which would seem to cast doubt on any argument that Paul had somehow altered his expectation before writing 1 Corinthians. The next step is to place Galatians between 2 Corinthians 1–9 and Romans, using comparisons in vocabulary and structure along lines first suggested by Lightfoot. The problematic nature of such arguments is visible when one looks at the exhaustive recent study by Udo Borse that uses precisely the same details to argue that Galatians was written between 2 Corinthians 1–9 and 2 Corinthians 10–13.[45] Then Buck and Taylor make detailed and convincing observations about the progression of the Corinthian controversy, placing 2 Corinthians 10–13 after 1 Corinthians but before Philippians or 2 Corinthians 1–9. Doctrinal "modifications" are adduced to place Colossians, Philemon, and Ephesians after Romans, and finally to place 2 Thessalonians before 1 Thessalonians.

The relative sequence of 2 Thessalonians, 1 Thessalonians, 1 Corinthians, 2 Corinthians 10–13, Philippians, 2 Corinthians 1–9, Galatians, Romans, Colossians, Philemon, Ephesians offers a chronological framework independent of the Book of Acts, an achievement whose methodical soundness is mitigated only by the difficulty in eliminating the element of subjectivity from development schemes.[46] An advance in theology for one scholar is a regression for the next, and the premise of organic theological development overlooks the highly situational character of the Pauline letters.[47]

When Buck and Taylor attempt to date the Thessalonian correspondence on the basis of references to the "restrainer" and the "lawless one," the results are untenable.[48] Placing the Apostolic Conference in 46 causes the seventeen year period mentioned in Galatians to be compressed to fourteen years, and results in placing Paul in Damascus too early to accommodate the Aretas date, which derives from the very Pauline letters they consider primary evidence. Finally, when Romans is placed in 47, just prior to the third Jerusalem visit to bring the offering, two anomalies arise: how can one reconcile the subsequent ministry on the eastern field including the writing of Colossians, Philippians, and Ephesians with the plan announced in Romans 15 to vacate the east and move on to Rome and Spain? and what is the motivation for the fourth Jerusalem visit that led to Paul's arrest? Buck and Taylor's acceptance of the spurious rationale of Acts 20:16 that Paul simply wanted to celebrate the Pentecost festival in Jerusalem is hardly convincing.[49] Further problems are caused when the data in Acts are coordinated with the epistle-based scheme. The famine trip and the Apostolic Conference are combined in the year 46, despite the lack of supporting evidence in Galatians; the hearing before Gallio is placed in the final three month visit to Corinth in the winter of 52–53, too late for Gallio's actual proconsulship there; and the Festus hearing is placed in 55, an improbably early choice. In light of the resultant necessity to skip over the irreconcilable dates relating to the Egyptian rebel and the departure from Philippi, one questions the accuracy of the claim that "we have at least the foundation of a consistent and workable chronology which accords with all the evidence of Acts and the letters."[50] The workability depends in part on how plausible one finds it to believe that in the two year period of 46–47 Paul made two separate trips to Jerusalem, had the conflict with Peter at Antioch, wrote four letters to the Corinthians, made the repeated trips reflected therein, and also found time to write 1 Thessalonians, Philippians, Galatians, and Romans.

## B. Galatians 2 Identical with Acts 18:22

In a series of articles and in *Chapters in a Life of Paul*, John Knox argued that the problem in Pauline chronology stems from the conflict between the five trips to Jerusalem reported by Luke and the three revealed in the letters.[51] Paul asserted in Galatians 1–2 that he had visited Jerusalem only twice since becoming a Christian: once, three years after his conversion to get acquainted with Peter (Gal. 1:18) and once again after fourteen years on the occasion of the Apostolic Conference (Gal. 2:1–10). The other letters reflect Paul's plan to visit Jerusalem once again to deliver the offering that he had gathered (1 Cor. 16:4; Rom. 15:25–32) in accordance with the promise made at the Apostolic Conference (Gal. 2:10). Acts, in contrast, presents five visits to Jerusalem, of which three correspond in motivation to the visits in the letters. There is the "acquaintance visit" of Acts 9:26–27, the "offering visit" in Acts 11:29–30 and the "conference visit" in Acts 15:1–29. The final two Jerusalem visits are presented without adequate motivation in Acts 18:22 and 21:15ff. Knox settles this conflict by giving the primary evidence in the letters priority over the secondary evidence in Acts and then sets about to discover why Luke inserted the two extra Jerusalem journeys. It reflects Luke's interest in picturing the relations between Paul and the mother church in harmonious terms, with Paul playing the role of a faithful and subordinate missionary who carries out Jerusalem's assignments. Since the conference visit as reported by Paul himself was in reality a profound struggle that ended with recognition of Paul's independence, Luke placed the event as early as possible to create the impression that difficulties had been solved early and finally.[52]

Knox's thesis is that the true setting for the Apostolic Conference is the strangely compressed account of the trip "up"[53] to Jerusalem in Acts 18:22. By linking the Galatians 2 conference with this trip in the later period of Paul's ministry, Knox escapes the necessity of positing seventeen empty years at the beginning of Paul's ministry and crowding virtually all that is known about his activity into the last few years. He then proceeds to show that the Jerusalem offering, designed to bridge the gap between the Palestinian and the Hellenistic churches,[54] provided the motivation for the final Jerusalem journey even though Luke erased all reference to it except for one detail he apparently overlooked (Acts 24:17). In order to account for the general knowledge in the early church that Paul had indeed brought an offering to Jerusalem, Luke placed such a trip in the early life of Paul in connection with a famine (Acts 11:27–30). Paul's explicit denial that he had made such a trip between the "acquaintance" journey and the "conference" journey is quite enough to overrule Luke's chronology at this point. This explains and eliminates the major conflicts between Acts and the letters, providing a three Jerusalem journey framework that could provide a workable basis for Pauline chronology. But the arbitrary elements in Knox's dating system caused its rejection by most scholars. He dates the conversion on grounds of probability alone "not earlier than A.D. 34 or 35."[55] Add three years to produce 37 for the acquaintance visit, and another fourteen to produce 51 for the date of the Apostolic Conference. Since Knox accepts 55 as the date of the Festus succession and interprets Acts 24:27 in the sense that Paul was in prison for two years prior to this date, the entire post–conference ministry is crowded into the short period between 51 and 53. Several other more glaring mistakes set most critics against Knox's scheme.[56] In the *Journal of Religion* article he equated the fourteen year span of Gal. 2:1 with the fourteen years mentioned in 2 Cor. 12:12, with the result that both letters had to be dated in the same year and the fourteen year span in Galatians would logically have to be counted from the conversion rather than from the last Jerusalem visit. Knox later admitted under the pressure of criticism "that the two intervals of fourteen years are probably a mere coincidence."[57] It was also a mistake to date the Corinthian ministry in the year 45, disregarding the Gallio inscription in an effort to avoid the fourteen "silent years" fallacy which, on a closer analysis of the results of his associating the conference with Acts 18:22, actually no longer existed.

Although unmentioned by Knox, there are several predecessors who identified Gal. 2:1 with Acts 18:22. Karl Georg Wieseler took this step in 1848 in order to eliminate the embarrassing conflicts between Galatians 2 and Acts 15.[58] Lacking the methodical penetration of Knox,[59] he retained all five Jerusalem journeys and produced a completely untenable chronology. With the Apostolic Conference in 54, he placed the conversion in 40 although he could easily have accommodated the entire seventeen year span and possibly fit in the Aretas data as well. The dating of the second Jerusalem journey in 45 and the third in 50 makes impossible any correlation with the Gallio proconsulship. Then with the conference in 54 and the arrest in Jerusalem in 58 he can scarcely fit in the crowded activities of the later period of Paul's ministry.

A step in the direction of Knox's methodical clarity was taken by Gustav Volkmar in 1884.[60] Affirming the priority of the Pauline letters over Lukan evidence, the acquaintance journey of Gal. 1:18 is identified with Acts 9:24 and the conference journey of Gal. 2:1 with Acts 22. The journeys in Acts 11 and 15 are viewed as doublets to the actual historical journeys. Volkmar pointed out Luke's compressed editing and the lack of motivation for the journey in Acts 18:22, but made it easy for his critics by positing two collection journeys late in Paul's career. The suggestion that Gal. 2:10 = Acts 24:17 and 1 Cor. 16:1–9 = Acts 20:4ff. was universally rejected and the significance of the hypothesis as a whole was first recognized by Ernst Barnikol in 1929.

Barnikol stressed more succinctly than Volkmar the methodical priority of the data from the letters over the Lukan five Jerusalem journey scheme.[61] The two extra Jerusalem journeys in Acts are explained as deriving from the Antioch tradition of expeditions with relief funds and negotiations concerning the Apostolic Decree; whether such traditions would have been included in the "we–source" as Barnikol argued is doubtful. But with the elimination of these two journeys a relatively workable chronology results, with the acquaintance journey in 40, the conference journey in 51–52 and the final collection journey in 57. Aside from the fact that Barnikol mistakenly subsumes the seventeen year span of Galatians into a fourteen year period, thereby getting Paul into Damascus a little too late to have encountered Aretas' ethnarch, this is the most successful chronological scheme ever proposed. It eliminates the time compression in the years before Paul's arrival in Corinth and allows one to fit in the rest of the ascertainable dates and time–spans. Although there is no detailed discussion of the individual journeys, of all the ascertainable dates, or the dating of the letters, this chronological framework would clearly correlate with several knowns: the Gallio inscription, the Claudius edict, the April 15, 57 departure from Philippi, the October, 59 departure from Fair Havens, the most probable date of the Festus/Felix tenure transition, and the time–span for Paul's execution. It would provide adequate time for the eighteen month Corinthian ministry, the two and a third year Ephesian ministry, the travels west to Illyrium, and the several Asian imprisonments. It is therefore regrettable that Barnikol's work has not received wider attention. But it is perhaps not surprising that so daring and non–apologetic a view should so soon have been forgotten amid the preponderance of compromise chronologies.

Gerd Lüdemann's *Habilitationsschrift* of 1977 is a suitable ending point because it pursues with such methodical clarity the Knox alternative.[62] A complex series of exegetical studies of the letters and Acts leads to a chronology based on the principle of the strict priority of evidence in the primary sources. He places the conversion in A.D. 30, the first Jerusalem journey in 33, two years after Paul's return to Damascus, and the second Jerusalem journey on the occasion of the Apostolic Conference in A.D. 47, 13 years after an indeterminate visit to Syria and Cilicia. On the theory that Acts 18 contains details from several visits, Lüdemann places the founding visit to Corinth in A.D. 41, assuming an early placement of the Claudius edict that forced Priscilla and Aquila out of Rome. The churches of Galatia, Philippi, and Thessalonica were founded prior to this, which naturally causes Lüdemann to disregard the Aretas datum. He seems on more solid ground in reconstructing from the letters a four year period of collection and letter writing activities after the Apostolic Conference. This brings him down to the winter of 51–52 when Paul wrote Romans from Corinth. It was on this occasion that the Gallio tradition was connected with Paul's visit. The chronology ends with the journey to Jerusalem in A.D. 52, leaving the reader with unanswered questions about the end of Paul's life.

There is no way to do Lüdemann's chronology justice without examining the detailed exegesis at key points. The early dating of the European ministry rests in part on interpreting "in the beginning of the gospel" in Phil. 4:15 as the actual start of Paul's independent mission just prior to A.D. 41.[63] He has difficulty explaining away the implication that Paul thus did not consider his work in Syria and Cilicia as the beginning of his ministry (Gal. 1:21). It is clear from the reference to his conversion in Gal. 1:16 that an independent apostolic consciousness was present from the start. Lüdemann is so eager to dispel the mistaken Lukan picture of Paul as a junior partner of Barnabas up to the time of the Apostolic Conference that he overinterprets what is surely a reference to the start of the Macedonian ministry in Phil. 4:15.[64] A second argument for the early mission in Macedonia develops out of the comparison of the eschatology of 1 Thessalonians and 1 Corinthians. That the latter presents a more refined concept of resurrection as transformation into spiritual bodies clearly differentiates it from the former. But to conclude that 7–8 years separate the two letters is claiming too much knowledge about the laws of mental development.[65] Given the situational qualities of the letters, it is impossible to draw sound conclusions about the precise periods required to evoke innovations.[66] It is obvious that the 7–8 year period is determined by the dates Lüdemann had already established for the founding of the Thessalonian congregation and the writing of 1 Corinthians.

The decisive arguments for multiple missions to Corinth derive from separating Acts 18:2–8 from 18:12–17. That the redactor mistakenly conflated traditions from widely separated visits is inferred primarily from references to Crispus as the ruler of the synagogue in 18:8 and Sosthenes in 18:16. Lüdemann rejects Wiefel's argument[67] that the conversion of Crispus could have caused the election of a new leader. He questions whether Wiefel presupposes "too strenuous an opposition between Judaism and Christianity" for this early period,[68] which strikes one as odd when Lüdemann argues for a full–scale controversy caused by Christian agitators in the Roman synagogues prior to A.D. 41.[69] Furthermore, Applebaum's definitive treatment of the organization of Jewish communities in the diaspora reveals a fluctuating pattern of leadership, with some synagogues having yearly terms of office and others having multiple leaders.[70]

Lüdemann's extensive analysis of the chronological details in Galatians begins with Hans Dieter Betz's theory of an "apologetic letter," in which Gal. 1:13–2:14 constitute the *narratio*.[71] According to classical rhetorical theory, such a recounting of a controversy aims not at a comprehensive story but at convincing an audience of the falsity of allegations, in this case derived from the Judaizers. Only the details explicitly related to the case at hand are allowed in a *narratio,* so that it is inappropriate to expect in the brief reference to "Syria and Cilicia" in Gal. 1:21 an exhaustive list of missionary stations. The point is that Paul did not travel to Jerusalem in the fourteen year interim. An even more decisive argument is derived from Quintilian's rhetorical handbook that a key event may sometimes be skipped over in a *narratio* to be treated later as the *causa,* the basis of the conflict. Thus Lüdemann argues that the conflict with Peter in Antioch described in Gal. 2:11ff. occurred before the Apostolic Conference described in Gal. 2:1–10, comprising the cause of the Conference itself. He is led to this conclusion by Conzelmann and Lindemann's assumption about an originally uncomplicated table fellowship between Jewish and gentile Christians being radically altered by the Council's division of the mission field.[72] The agreement in Gal. 2:9 that Paul would go to the gentiles and Peter to the "circumcised" would presumably have eliminated such solidarity. Lüdemann goes on to suggest that the Apostolic Decree was agreed upon by mixed congregations such as Antioch, but that Paul as a representative of strictly Hellenistic congregations did not have to submit. Hence the inclusion of the Decree in the Acts 15 account of the conference reflects the Antioch Source, because the Decree pertained specifically to that city. The underlying issue of the Apostolic Conference was therefore the tension in mixed congregations, in the context of which the demand for circumcision was simply a radical solution.[73]

Lüdemann's premise throughout this discussion is that Paul represented a strictly Hellenistic branch of the church, which does not tally well with the evidence concerning the mixed composition of the Corinthian congregation. What appears logical to Lüdemann, Conzelmann, and Lindemann on the basis of Gal. 2:9 does not seem to have been felt in the early church, and there is no evidence that Paul thought the agreement at the Apostolic Conference eliminated table fellowship between circumcised and uncircumcised members of the church. Furthermore, if one were to accept the suggested reversal between the Antioch conflict and the Apostolic Conference, Paul's entire defense in the *narratio* would collapse, violating the Quintilian premise on which the reversal supposedly took place. After arguing for coexistence at Antioch, Paul would then have agreed to racial and cultural separatism at the Conference, and hence to a permanent abandonment of intercultural fellowship. Rather than demonstrating Paul's clear defense of the faith in Antioch, the placement of this episode as the *causa* would have shown that he, rather than Peter and Barnabas, was guilty of insincerity (Gal. 2:13).[74] Finally, the natural, antithetical sense of *hote de* in Gal. 2:11 does not denote the kind of historical flashback Lüdemann suggests.[75]

The negative results of this evaluation do not eliminate the permanent contributions of Lüdemann's work. He provides 1) conclusive proof of Paul's independent mission prior to the Apostolic Conference, thus refuting Acts' placement of the conference. Lüdemann stresses Paul's independent assumption of the obligation to organize the Jerusalem collection and infers from Gal. 2:5–8 that Paul relies on knowledge within the Galatian congregation of his independent mission. He shows that the details in Corinthians imply a founding of the congregation prior to the conference. Lüdemann develops 2) a conclusive argument that the Jerusalem journey reflected in Acts 18:18–23 is the logical spot for placing the Apostolic Conference. His redaction critical conclusions tally with those reached independently in this study, that Acts 18:18d, 19b–21a are editorial insertions, and that Jerusalem journeys number 2 and number 3 in Acts 11 and 15 are triplets of the journey reported in Acts 18:22. The correlation of travel details in Acts 15–18 with the schedule reconstructed from the Pauline letters proves that the conference reported in Galatians 2 fits only at Acts 18:22. His study shows 3) that when methodical priority is given to the letters and the redaction critical method is applied to Acts, the resultant details appear at times to be reliable. "After the elimination of the Lukan redaction, these accounts often contain old and worthwhile tradition."[76]

Despite these contributions, the weaknesses of the Lüdemann chronology are substantial. Having followed his reading of the secondary evidence in Acts 18 to posit an extremely early founding of the Corinthian congregation in A.D. 41, he is forced to disregard the primary evidence in 2 Corinthians 11 concerning the escape from Aretas. This violation of Lüdemann's methodology leads to serious consequences. 1) With the European mission starting so soon, the Apostolic Conference has to be placed in A.D. 37, which requires a paring back of the fourteen and three year periods mentioned in Galatians. He argues for such a reduction on grounds of probability, and links the periods to the return to Damascus in Gal. 1:17 and the mission to Syria and Cilicia in 1:21, but the problem of time compression is obvious. This causes 2) an improbably early conversion date of A.D. 30, disregarding the most likely alternatives for the date of the crucifixion. He is forced to opt for the rather unlikely date of A.D. 27 for Jesus' execution.

Although Lüdemann does not work out the subsequent details, the final trip to Jerusalem in A.D. 52 eliminates the possibility of correlation with 3) the Felix/Festus transfer in 59 or 60, 4) the probable *terminus a quo* for the Egyptian rebel in 57, 5) the *terminus a quo* for encountering Ananias the high priest in 53, 6) the late departure from Fair Havens on the Rome trip, and 7) the departure from Philippi on April 15, 54 or 57. None of these details derived from Acts bears decisive weight in and of itself, but the cumulative weight of discrepancies with the data we are using as criteria for evaluating chronological hypotheses is rather serious. Finally 8) the chronologist is left with the question of what occurred between Paul's presumed arrival in Rome in the early 50s and the probable date of his execution in the early 60s. Is Lüdemann prepared to follow the logic of his chronology and claim that Paul was executed by Claudius? or in the early months of Nero's reign? or that Paul was released and missionized in Spain for a decade? None of these options would be congruent with the methodology Lüdemann pursues through most of his work.

The final points to be made are that the mistakes in Lüdemann's chronology are correctable, and that the permanent contributions of his work remain intact. He has achieved an important methodological breakthrough, using the traditional tools of historical critical exegesis. That some of his most important conclusions should have been so similar to the ones achieved by the application of the experimental method in this study serves to increase the credibility of the Acts 18:22 = Galatians 2 alternative. It is an easy step to move from Lüdemann's study to a tenable solution to the problem of Pauline chronology. (For additional chronologies of this type, see note 77.)

GENERAL CONCLUSIONS

Viewed from an experimental perspective, what conclusions emerge from this review of previous chronologies? Despite the fact that scholars occasionally differed in the establishment of a date, notably in the complicated questions of the Felix/Festus tenure, this research is more than a comedy of errors. It is a moving demonstration of the irreducible internal pressures caused by combining the ascertainable data with the traditional Lukan framework. Whenever Acts 15 is identified with Galatians

2, the tension between the date of the conversion and the arrival in Corinth causes pressure on both the seventeen year span and the Jerusalem–Corinth itinerary; it usually forces one to overlook the Aretas date. Whenever Acts 11 is identified with Galatians 2, the tension between the conversion and the famine causes a radical reduction of the seventeen year span, and often produces the additional anomaly of a double Apostolic Conference. It inevitably causes the elimination of the Aretas date. Neither of the traditional compromise approaches allows sufficient time for the complicated travels, ministries, and imprisonments to take place before the closing of Paul's eastern missionary activities in the spring of 57. Luke's insertion of extra Jerusalem journeys causes irreducible pressures. Every conceivable experiment has been tried, repeatedly, to overcome one or more of these problems. The result of reducing pressure at one point is to increase it elsewhere, causing the violation of some other ascertainable date or time-span. It is therefore appropriate to conclude that the traditional compromises between the ascertainable data and the Lukan framework of Jerusalem journeys are all unworkable.[78] Additional experiments along that line should be abandoned, since every conceivable option has already been tested and found lacking.

In light of the failure of the compromise chronologies, it would appear that the epistle oriented approaches should be more viable. But while they are methodically preferable, the chronologies based exclusively on evidence within the letters have not been successful. They do not provide the degree of precision required to work out detailed itineraries and interlocking time-spans. And in the degree to which they rely upon theories of developmental sequence within the Pauline letter corpus, such chronologies are open to the charge of subjectivity.

The most promising of the epistle oriented type of chronology are those that concentrate on eliminating the discrepancies in the number of Jerusalem journeys. The Knox/Barnikol/Lüdemann combination of the Acts 18:22 journey with that described in Galatians 2 looks like the most suitable avenue for further exploration. By retaining the strict methodical priority of primary over secondary evidence, this approach appears to offer the best way to incorporate the ascertainable dates and time-spans from Acts. It can eliminate the pressure between the seventeen year span and the Aretas datum by placing the Apostolic Conference after the arrival in Corinth. By eliminating the extra Jerusalem journey that Acts inserted between the Apostolic Conference and final delivery of the Jerusalem collection, it allows time in the period between the conference and the departure from Philippi in A.D. 57 for the extensive travels reflected in Philippians, Corinthians, and Romans. The refinement of this experimental option is the logical next step in the quest for a solution to the problem of Pauline chronology. To develop a sound basis for this experiment, it is necessary to summarize the major causes of the chronological problem.

# CHAPTER V

# THE MAJOR CAUSES OF THE CHRONOLOGICAL DILEMMA

The curious dilemma of Pauline chronology is that although the ascertainable date-frames and time-spans can be established with a relative degree of certainty, scholars are no closer to a consensus now than they were a hundred years ago about how to fit the data together. The chronologies we have reviewed contain a bewildering series of variations, and in the midst of constant fluctuation many of the ascertainable details are overlooked or adjusted. In view of the integrity and diligence with which able scholars have labored over the problem, this is incongruous. Such manipulations have not been a matter of choice. They are the results of conflicts within the evidence provided by Acts and the letters. The problem cannot be solved by an additional genial compromise, but only by the exposure and elimination of these conflicts. An analysis of previous research indicates where the major trouble spots are.

## THE CONFLICTS BETWEEN GALATIANS 2 AND ACTS 11–15

Since the beginning of chronological research, the effort has been to find a workable compromise between the diverging reports in Galatians 2 and Acts 11–15. Although Paul explicitly states that he had visited the church in Jerusalem only once prior to the Apostolic Conference, Luke reports two separate visits to Jerusalem, once shortly after his conversion (Acts 9:26–30) and one at the time of a famine in Judea (Acts 11:27–30; 12:25). As if this contradiction between Luke and Paul were not difficult enough, the account of the famine relief is complicated by Luke's implication that it took place before Herod Agrippa's death in 44 (Acts 12: 20–23), whereas we know from secular sources that the famine did not take place until after this date. It is further complicated by Luke's report that the first missionary journey began after the delivery of the famine relief (Acts 13:1ff.); since the Apostolic Conference could scarcely have taken place before the first missionary journey conducted jointly by Paul and Barnabas, the possibilities of solving this conflict by simply conflating the accounts in Acts 11 and 15 would seem to be severely limited.

Nevertheless every conceivable hypothesis has been set forth in the effort to solve these contradictions.[1] Cadoux,[2] Bruce,[3] and others[4] identify Acts 11 with Galatians 2, under the assumption that the meeting which Paul describes took place prior to the Apostolic Conference reported in Acts 15. Aside from the fact that the visit in Galatians 2 appears to have little in common with that reported in Acts 11, this theory requires that the double-purposed visit to Jerusalem take place in A.D. 48. This forces one to compress the first missionary journey into the improbable span of less than a year so as to place the Acts 15 conference in the year 49. Furthermore it forces one to make the highly improbable assumption that Galatians could have been written after A.D. 49 without containing any reference to the second conference which had most recently taken place. Another compromise was worked out by Goguel, who identifies the Apostolic Conference in Acts 15 and Galatians 2 with the visit in Acts 11, placing the combined visit in A.D. 43-44.[5] This results in an improbable placing of the first missionary journey after the Apostolic Conference which dealt with the implications of precisely such a successful gentile mission, and it forces Goguel to reject Paul's statements in Gal. 1:18 and 2:1 that he was converted seventeen years prior to the Conference.[6]

Similar hypotheses by Meyer[7] and Schwartz[8] set the Apostolic Conference in A.D. 43, the time of the journey in Acts 11, but they assume that Luke was mistaken about the reason for the visit by Paul and Barnabas. This produces intolerable pressure on the seventeen year span between conversion and conference, and despite Meyer's compression of this into fifteen years, he cannot make a convincing case that Paul was converted in A.D. 28. The hypothesis worked out by Lake is no more successful,[9] for in identifying the famine trip with the Apostolic Conference and setting the resultant visit in A.D. 46, he places the Conference too early to accommodate the required seventeen year span.[10] Jeremias combines the famine trip and the Apostolic Conference, placing them in 48, but his pivotal dating of this on the basis of the Sabbath year is finally undemonstrable.[11] Dockx combines the famine and conference trip accounts by means of a problematic literary hypothesis. With Benoît, he suggests that Acts 13-14 were inserted into a previously unified account of a Jerusalem journey.[12] A major impediment is that Acts 15:5ff. and Gal. 2:1ff. relate the purpose of the Jerusalem meeting in terms of a conflict over gentile circumcision, while Dockx's theory would retain the delivering of famine relief as the primary motivation. The less radical solution offered by Zahn, Plooij, and Guthrie is no more satisfactory because in dating the famine visit in 44 or 46 and the Apostolic Conference in 48 or 49, they must assume that Paul did not mean what he said about his failure to visit Jerusalem more than once prior to the Apostolic Conference.[13] Parker takes Paul seriously at this point, eliminating the journey of Acts 9 instead of Acts 11, implausibly identifying the latter with the acquaintance visit of Gal. 1:18.[14]

These hypotheses show the futility of compromising between Acts and the Pauline letters. The evidence from Galatians 1–2 and the ascertainable dates of the famine and the crucifixion simply cannot be reconciled with Luke's account of the famine visit in Acts 11. Paul's comment in Gal. 1:20 that he was "unknown by face" to the Judean churches speaks decisively against the famine visit.[15] Furthermore, the analysis of the sources indicated that this early Jerusalem journey is an integral part of Luke's theological framework. The author of Acts pictures Paul as closely tied with the Jerusalem church so as to maintain the continuity of the salvation-history. Since the story of the second Jerusalem journey is theologically motivated and irreconcilable with the ascertainable dates, one must conclude that it is unhistorical.[16] Its elimination may make it possible to realign this earlier period of Paul's activities in such a way as to allow for all of the ascertainable details. This is at any rate a first step in following the methodical guideline of granting the ascertainable dates precedence over the Lukan framework.

## THE TIME COMPRESSION BETWEEN CONVERSION AND CONFERENCE

Paul's arrival in Corinth on the second missionary expedition (Acts 18:1) can be reckoned on the basis of Acts 18:11 and the Gallio inscription to have fallen between the winter of 49–50 and 50–51. Most researchers have chosen the earlier date as more probable. This ascertainable date is one of the two poles between which the date of the Apostolic Conference fluctuates, the other being the date of the crucifixion that provides the *terminus a quo* for reckoning the date of the conversion seventeen years before the conference. Most contemporary chronologists set the date of the Apostolic Conference either in 48[17] or 49.[18] Taken by itself, this slight fluctuation appears unimportant. But when one notes that Harnack set the conference as early as 47[19] and that both Meyer and Lake place the beginning of the second missionary journey in the same year,[20] one's curiosity is naturally aroused. What pressure is there to push back the beginning of the second missionary journey and the Apostolic Conference which immediately preceded it to 47 or 48 when the seventeen year time-span demands a date of 49, 50, or even 51, so as to provide time for the development of the early church prior to Paul's conversion?

The detailed reconstruction of the timetable between Jerusalem and Corinth on the so-called "second missionary journey"[21] provides the answer. When one calculates the 3497 kilometer journey by land and sea and takes account of the visits to Antioch, Cilicia, Derbe, Lystra, Iconium, Pisidian Antioch, the North Galatian cities of Pessimus, Germa, and/or Ancyra, and the stays in Troas, Philippi, Thessalonica, Beroea, and Athens, it is clear that three to four years must be allotted. This would match the pace of Paul's later ministry as reflected in the authentic letters and the "we-account" sections in Acts. Unless there is clear evidence to the contrary, it is methodically inappropriate to assume that the pace of travel and missionary work was miraculously rapid on this particular expedition that resulted in the founding of so many of Paul's important congregations.

The dilemma is obvious. If Paul arrived in approximately January of A.D. 50 at Corinth, the departure from Jerusalem after the Apostolic conference must have taken place in 46 or 47. The result is that there is clearly no longer room for the seventeen year span between the conference and Paul's conversion. This is the second cause of the problem in Pauline chronology: there is not enough time between the crucifixion in 30 or 33 and the arrival in Corinth in 49-50 for the second missionary expedition, the Apostolic Conference, the escape from Aretas, the conversion, and the seventeen year span. This chronic state of time compression indicates that something is amiss within the data.

## THE PROBLEM OF THE LUKAN FRAMEWORK

Unless one is willing to sacrifice or manipulate the ascertainable dates and time-spans, there remains only one avenue in determining what causes these insoluble dilemmas. Both in the question of relating Acts 11–15 with Galatians 2 and in the dilemma of time compression between the conversion and the Apostolic Conference, the Lukan framework of five Jerusalem journeys plays a key role. In the latter case, it is obvious that traditional chronologies have been entirely dependent on Luke for the sequence of first missionary journey / Apostolic Conference / second missionary journey. As noted above, there is a specific theological motivation behind this framework, namely, that of making the independent missionary activity of the second expedition, when Barnabas was absent, appear to be the direct consequence of the Apostolic Conference at Jerusalem. Not only is Paul's independence thereby supported by the Jerusalem pillars, but also the specific goal of the second journey is pictured as related to the distribution of the Jerusalem decree. By placing the Apostolic Conference before the second missionary journey, Luke can make Paul appear to be a faithful representative of the Jerusalem centered salvation–history. As F. F. Bruce puts it in defending Acts' version, ". . . there is ground for believing that Jerusalem filled an important role in Paul's eschatological thinking. . . . Not only did the gospel first go out into all the world from Jerusalem; Jerusalem . . . would be the scene of its glorious consummation."[22]

There is of course no *a priori* reason why a connection with Lukan theology proves something to be historically false; the salvation–history framework may have attached itself to a perfectly neutral historical event and left it in its original sequence. Yet the fact that the Lukan framework is impossible to reconcile with the ascertainable dates and time–spans in two areas of decisive significance gives one adequate grounds to call it into question. It is quite probable that the imposition of this framework is responsible for the constant pressure to date the crucifixion as early as possible and the arrival of Gallio as late as possible. It has given rise to the fantastic series of conjectures to reduce the seventeen year span to fifteen, thirteen, eleven, or even four years. The analysis of the research therefore confirms the conclusions of Chapter I, that the Lukan framework is the most vulnerable point in Pauline chronology. The abandonment of this framework is thus a practical as well as a methodical necessity. As Solomon Zeitlin put it in discussing the conflict between the number of Jerusalem journeys in Acts and Galatians, ". . . a historian who is not motivated by theology will reject Acts and accept the Epistle to the Galatians."[23] This sustains the conclusion of Chapter IV, that the methodical route to an experimental solution is to refine the approach popularized by John Knox that addresses itself so directly to the distortions caused by the Lukan framework.

# CHAPTER VI

# THE EXPERIMENTAL HYPOTHESIS

To refine the Barnikol/Knox hypothesis of a three Jerusalem journey framework, an experimental approach is required. Although it has been possible to establish time-spans and probable *termini a quo* and *ad quem* for a number of dates, there is no *a priori* basis for placing these spans in first century history or setting precise points within the probable limits for specific dates. Given the intense debate on each issue, one cannot state beforehand which of these details can successfully be incorporated in a chronology. To overcome this dilemma, an experimental system of date-ranges and time-spans is proposed. These have been placed on parallel graphs denoting the months of the first century calendar. (See Graph of Dates and Time-Spans at the end of this volume.) If it is true that history is unrepeatable, the graphs of time-spans should interlock with the graph of ascertainable date-ranges at only one point in the life of a historical figure like Paul. The task is to discover where the interlock occurs. And the test is whether all of the ascertainable data can successfully be placed within the resultant chronology. Once the points of interlock have been designated, the chronology can be reckoned out in precise detail, making the verification of the experiment possible. Although it may strike some students of Pauline chronology as overly presumptuous to calculate the precise implications of the interlock, this is the only basis on which the experiment can be replicated.

## THE FRAMEWORK OF TIME-SPANS

The Barnikol/Knox hypothesis offers a framework of three Jerusalem journeys interspersed with missionary activities and other historical events. All of the data for this framework come from the primary evidence in the Pauline letters as opposed to the secondary evidence in the Book of Acts. In a recent dictionary article, John C. Hurd, Jr. has confirmed the methodological correctness of this epistle oriented approach.[1] He works out a basic framework of dates which is adapted below, with the addition of time–spans mentioned in Galatians.

> Conversion (Gal. 1:15–16; 1 Cor. 15:8)
> Three Year Time-Span (Gal. 1:18)
> First Jerusalem Visit (Gal. 1:18–19)
> Missionary Activity (Gal. 1:21)
> Fourteen Year Time-Span (Gal. 2:1)
> Second Jerusalem Visit (Gal. 2:1–10)
> Missionary Work, Including Collection
> (1 Cor. 16:1–8, etc.)
> Third Jerusalem Visit (Rom. 15:25–33)
> Imprisonment and Execution

The key elements in this framework are the three year and the fourteen year spans antedating the second Jerusalem journey. They provide a seventeen year period with the conversion at one end and the Apostolic Conference in Jerusalem at the other. During this period the evidence in Galatians implies that Paul made only one Jerusalem journey, designated on the graph as "First Jerusalem Visit," which means that the extra Jerusalem journey in Acts 11 had been eliminated from the framework. Since the Barnikol/Knox hypothesis identifies the second Jerusalem visit at the time of the Apostolic Conference with that described in Acts 18:22, this framework in effect also eliminates the third of Acts' five Jerusalem journeys.

## THE SEVENTEEN YEAR INTERLOCK

The logical place to begin the process of positing a satisfactory interlock between the framework of time–spans and the graph of ascertainable date–frames is at the end of the seventeen year period, the time of the Apostolic Conference. According to the Barnikol/Knox hypothesis which I am extending, the conference came after the Corinthian ministry. Paul appeared before the proconsul Gallio in a judicial proceeding (Acts 18:12–17) which in all probability occurred at the end of the eighteen month Corinthian ministry (Acts 18:1).[2] This means that a one year time–span corresponding to the length of time Gallio was in office can be established eighteen months prior to Gallio's tenure from July 1, 51 through July 1, 52.[3] During this one year period from January 1, 50 to January 1, 51, Paul began his ministry in Corinth. In the unlikely event that the judicial hearing occurred toward the beginning of the Corinthian ministry, the latest possible *terminus ad quem* for Paul's arrival would be July 1, 52.

This date–range can be closely correlated with Paul's encounter with Priscilla and Aquila at the beginning of the Corinthian ministry (Acts 18:2–3). As we determined in Chapter II, their recent arrival from Rome in the wake of expulsion by Claudius' edict establishes a narrow date-range for the encounter with Paul. It must have taken place between March of A.D. 49 and March of A.D. 50. Taken by themselves, neither of these date–ranges allows a very precise chronological inference. But when the principle of chronological interlock is applied, it is immediately apparent that the two date–ranges overlap with a rather narrow margin. Since the latest Paul could have met Priscilla and Aquila was March, 51, and the earliest Paul could have arrived in Corinth to appear before Gallio at the end of an eighteen month ministry was January, 51, it follows that Paul's arrival in Corinth fell somewhere in this three month period. A three year range is thereby narrowed down to the chronologically useful period from January–March, 51, for Paul's arrival.

When one calculates the travel time from Corinth to Jerusalem for the Apostolic Conference which followed the eighteen month Corinthian ministry, the date–range is narrowed even further. The details of the reconstruction are as follows. From the account in Acts 18 it is clear that Luke knows nothing to report for the period between the Gallio hearing and the departure for Jerusalem for what we surmise was the Apostolic Conference. The author contents himself with saying that Paul remained in Corinth "some days" (Acts 18:18) and then departed. Most interpreters have assumed that the eighteen month period (Acts 18:11) referred to the total visit and that Paul left within a few days after the judicial proceeding.[4] Paul sailed with Priscilla and Aquila, stopping in Ephesus to drop them off (Acts 18:18–19). Among the curious features of this compressed account of the journey is that Paul traveled alone, thus breaking his custom of taking companions and helpers on every trip.[5] He had left Silas and Timothy somewhere in Macedonia (Acts 18:5) and Aquila and Priscilla to prepare the way for a new center of work at Ephesus.[6] It is possible to explain this unusual element of the journey by means of information Paul himself provides, that he went up to Jerusalem with Barnabas and Titus (Gal. 2:1). They could have met at some predetermined point such as Cyprus or Caesarea. Or, as seems more likely, Paul sailed to Syria, i.e., Antioch, as Acts 18:18 reveals. There he met Titus and

Barnabas by prearrangement and traveled to Jerusalem with the support of the Antioch church, which had recently been troubled by the circumcision agitators (Acts 15:1-2). Whether the trip from Antioch to Jerusalem was made by land (Acts 15:3) or by ship (Acts 18:22), it is clear that Luke means to imply with *anabas* (Acts 18:22) the journey "up" to Jerusalem.[7] So when one reckons three weeks for a sea journey from Corinth to Antioch,[8] a week long interval in Antioch, and a month for a leisurely overland journey to Jerusalem, the arrival there could easily occur in September if Paul had departed from Corinth in mid-July, the earliest possible date for his departure. Taking the sea route from Antioch to Caesarea would have allowed arrival in Jerusalem for the Apostolic Conference as early as August. The presence of prearrangements for this crucially important conference[9] makes it unlikely that the trip took place after the normal traveling season was over. Thus the arrival in Jerusalem was probably not after the end of October. The Apostolic Conference therefore took place some time between August and October of A.D. 51.

At first glance the establishment of a three month date-range for the Apostolic Conference would appear to have gained little in the direction of precision. But when the principle of chronological interlock is applied, the three month period diminishes to less than a month. If Paul had begun his ministry in Corinth as late as March of 50, his hearing before Gallio eighteen months later would have occurred in September, 52, making it highly unlikely that he could have made travel arrangements to arrive in Jerusalem by the October deadline. In light of the fact that Paul could scarcely have appeared before Gallio and departed less than two weeks after the proconsul's arrival on July 1, 51, the date-range of the departure for the Apostolic Conference is narrowed to the period from mid-July through the latter part of August of 51.

The method of chronological interlocking is illustrated even more decisively when one calculates the fourteen year interval between the Apostolic Conference and the date of Paul's first Jerusalem journey. This can be dated, as shown in Chapter II, on the basis of Paul's reference to an escape from the ethnarch of Aretas (2 Cor. 11:32-33) which preceded it. Aretas' control of Damascus was possible only between the summer of A.D. 37 and the year 39. Paul's first Jerusalem visit of two weeks' duration (Gal. 1:18) could not therefore have occurred prior to the late summer or fall of A.D. 37. When one calculates a full fourteen year span backwards from the August-October date-range in A.D. 51, the interlock is exact. If the Apostolic Conference had occurred before August of 51, Paul could not have been threatened by the ethnarch of Aretas in Damascus fourteen years earlier.

The exact interlock of these three date–spans and the fourteen year time–span is a decisive indication of the workability of the new hypothesis. It reduces to a matter of weeks the range of chronological probability in the period between Paul's first Jerusalem journey and the Apostolic Conference. It makes possible the establishment of the date of Paul's conversion three years prior to the first Jerusalem journey in the year 34, well within the range of probability, whether one sets the crucifixion in A.D. 30 or 33. If Paul's reference in Gal. 1:18 is taken to be three full years, his conversion occurred between August and October of 34. The preliminary results of the interlock are as follows:

Conversion ........................ August–October, 34
Three Year Time–Span ......................... 34–37
Escape from Aretas ................. August–October, 37
First Jerusalem Visit ................ August–October, 37
Fourteen Year Time–Span ....................... 37–51
Paul's Arrival in Corinth .......... January–February, 50
Departure from Corinth ....... Mid–July–Late August, 51
Apostolic Conference .............. August–October, 51

An even more precise designation of dates is possible when one correlates this framework with a final fragment of evidence that no chronology since the time of Adolf von Harnack has been able to incorporate successfully. As recounted in Chapter II, he correlated early Christian and Gnostic references to eighteen months of resurrection occurences with 1 Cor. 15:8, producing a date of October 3 or 8, 34, for Paul's conversion. No one would wish to accord such a datum deriving from tenuous oral tradition a pivotal role in NT chronology. Yet its correlation with the new hypothesis is stunning. It falls precisely within the date–range for the conversion that resulted from the interlock between the three well-documented dates and the seventeen year time–span. It is hard to believe that mere chance could account for so precise a fit in details deriving from such a wide variety of sources. The probability of a workable conjunction between the Harnack datum and the other three dates with a seventeen year time-span over a twenty year period is 1 to 474,591.[10] The fact that Harnack's inference correlates so exactly with the chronological interlock provides it a kind of systemic authenticity. The result of accepting such a datum is that the conversion can be set in early October, 34, and the first Jerusalem visit in October of 37, with the escape from Aretas immediately before this.

The chronological implications at the other end of the seventeen year time–span can also be worked out. The date of the Apostolic Conference which formerly had the date–range of August–October, 51, can be narrowed down to the four week period at the end of this range. If the conference fell in October, 51, the departure from Corinth could easily have come in August, thus allowing adequate time for the hearing before Gallio to have occurred in the first month, as opposed to the first week of his tenure beginning July 1, 51. Reckoning backwards eighteen months from August, 51, brings us to February, 50, as the probable time of Paul's arrival in Corinth. The results are tabulated in the following summary:

Conversion ......................... October 3 or 8, 34
Three Year Time–Span .......... October, 34–October, 37
First Jerusalem Journey .................... October, 37
Fourteen Year Span ............ October, 37–October, 51
Paul's Arrival in Corinth ................. February, 50
Departure from Corinth .................... August, 51
Apostolic Conference ...................... October, 51

THE PHILIPPI TO ROME INTERLOCK

The second chronological interlock resulting from combining the Barnikol/Knox hypothesis with the ascertainable date–ranges relates to the imprisonment at Caesarea which began after Paul's third Jerusalem journey. The time–span in this instance comes from Acts 24:27. "But when two years had elapsed, Felix was succeeded by Porcius Festus; and desiring to do the Jews a favor, Felix left Paul in prison." Redaction critics have not detected a theological motivation in this time–span reference, and the commentators who are not under chronological pressure at this point leave no doubt that the two years pertain to Paul's imprisonment rather than to Felix's tenure in office.[11] Nevertheless the fact that this time–span derives from a secondary source makes it less reliable than the seventeen year span used in the first interlock. The workability of the two year span can be tested, however, by correlation with a series of other date–frames that derive from independent sources.

The crucial dates for the Philippi to Rome interlock are the departure from Philippi and the July 1 accession of Festus in Caesarea. Ramsay and Plooij combined astronomical tables with the travel details in Acts 20:6-11, resulting in two possible dates for the departure from Philippi: April 15, 54, or April 15, 57.[12] When correlated with the most probable date for Festus replacing Felix as procurator, July 1, 59,[13] it is obvious that the latter date is more feasible. The interlock of the two year span between the April 15, 57, departure from Philippi and the July 1, 59 accession of Festus is rather precise when one calculates the travel arrangements in detail. It is possible to reconstruct the journey from Philippi to Jerusalem in such a way as to have Paul arrive in time for the Pentecost celebration on May 29, 57, assuming that he succeeded in achieving the goal imputed to him in Acts 20:16.[14] But there are redaction critical as well as historical reasons to doubt that Paul shared the urgency Luke implies to schedule his visits at the times of Jewish festivals. The theme of Paul's presumed fulfillment of the Jewish law is an important facet in Luke's effort to gloss over the conflict over the law between groups in the early church and between Paul and his Jewish adversaries.[15] Luke avoids direct references to the offering, which was Paul's motivation for the trip to Jerusalem, substituting the probably spurious motif of the Pentecost celebration.[16] As noted earlier, the reference to haste in sailing past Ephesus (Acts 20:17) is illogical in light of the resultant necessity of waiting for the Ephesian elders to arrive in Miletus. That Paul actually arrived in Jerusalem for the Pentecost celebration is unlikely in view of Luke's silence about whether the desire expressed in Acts 20:16 was fulfilled. And in light of Paul's recent escape from an assassination plot on a ship full of Jerusalem pilgrims bound for a temple festivity,[17] it seems unlikely that he would have sought to schedule his visit during Pentecost when the zealous crowds would be at their height. One must keep in mind that Paul's aim was to continue west with the mission and not to die at the hands of the Sicariats in Jerusalem. The arrival in Jerusalem was thus probably after Pentecost, so that the imprisonment following the temple riot (Acts 21:27ff.) would have begun in the summer of A.D. 57. The arrival probably took place in June or early July.

The correlation between the two year Caesarean imprisonment and the arrival in Jerusalem would bring the chronology to midsummer, 59. At this point the details in Acts 25:1-6 can be placed rather precisely in the first two weeks of July. The hearing before Festus would fall in mid-July and the hearing before Agrippa in August (Acts 25:13-26:32).

The departure from Caesarea under Roman guard would fall in late August or early September, 59.

This interlock is confirmed by several other date–ranges that correlate very smoothly. The tenure of Ananias the high priest, whom Paul encountered on this final Jerusalem visit (Acts 23:2; 24:1), ran from A.D. 53–59.[18] The reference to the Egyptian rebel in Acts 21:38 provided a probable *terminus a quo* of A.D. April, 56, which correlates even more precisely.[19] The interlock allows an arrival in Rome well before the *terminus ad quem* of A.D. 61 as calculated by Plooij on the basis of the reference to a single prefect in the Western Text of Acts 28:16.[20] It allows a plausible reconstruction of the hearings at Caesarea and the travel arrangements reported in Acts 27:1–8, allowing for the late departure from Fair Havens in October 15, 59.[21] This would place the shipwreck on October 18, the landing on Malta on November 2, and the end of the three month stay on Malta in February.[22] Paul's arrival in Rome would therefore fall in late February or early March of 60.[23]

The conclusive anchor in the Philippi to Rome interlock is the correlation with the *terminus a quo* for Paul's execution in A.D. 62. When one calculates the "two whole years" of imprisonment in his own quarters in Rome (Acts 28:30) followed by his execution, the margin of overlap between the two time–spans is reduced to the month of March, A.D. 62. In this case the principle of chronological interlock has reduced the two and a half year period, in which Paul was probably executed,[24] to a chronologically useful period of a single month. Assuming an execution at the conclusion of the two year imprisonment, the end of Paul's career fell in March, 62.

The smooth correlation of all these date–frames with the chronological interlock raises the probability of its experimental adequacy. The odds against these dates and time–frames correlating in a purely accidental manner over a twelve year time period are 14,170 to 1.[25] The results of the second interlock are tabulated below:

Departure from Philippi . . . . . . . . . . . . . . . . . . . . April 15, 57
Arrival in Jerusalem . . . . . . . . . . . . . . . . . . . . . . . . June, 57
Two Year Caesarean Imprisonment . . . . . June, 57–June, 59
Hearing Before Festus . . . . . . . . . . . . . . . . . . . . Mid–July, 59
Departure from Fair Havens . . . . . . . . . . . . . October 15, 59
Three Months on Malta . . November, 59–early February, 60
Arrival in Rome . . . . . . . . . . . . . . . . . . . . . . . . Early March, 60
Execution of Paul . . . . . . . . . . . . . . . . . . . . . . . . March, 62

## THE ADVANTAGES OF THE NEW HYPOTHESIS

The application of the principle of chronological interlocking establishes the dates of all three Jerusalem journeys, and leaves open the time from October, 51, to April, 57, for the travels and letter writing that can be reconstructed from the primary evidence in the Pauline epistles. As the detailed analysis of Paul's communications with each congregation to which he addressed letters can show, there is adequate time here for the Ephesian ministry, the extensive communications with Corinth, the Ephesian and Asian imprisonments, and the mission west as far as Illyrium. In the period before the Apostolic Conference, there is ample space for the three to four year itinerary from Jerusalem to Corinth and for a two year expedition through Cyprus, Pamphylia, and South Galatia. In the graph of dates and time–spans, all of the miscellaneous seasonal references and dates can be incorporated with ease. Thus the major requirement for an experimental hypothesis is met: all of the ascertainable date–frames, time–spans, and seasonal indications can be accommodated without stretch or pressure.

The new hypothesis provides the basis for solving several important problems related to the dating of the letters. If the Apostolic Conference took place at the end of the second missionary journey, as the Barnikol/Knox hypothesis assumes, then the relationship between Thessalonians and Galatians can be clarified. Heretofore it had always been puzzling that the Thessalonian letters which were written shortly after the traditional date of the Apostolic Conference in the midst of the second missionary journey bore no reflection whatever of the nomistic struggle. The puzzle was compounded by the fact that Galatians, which traditionally is placed several years after the Apostolic Conference, deals with the nomistic problem as if it were still very recent and refers to the conference as if it belonged to the very recent past. With the Apostolic Conference set between the second and third missionary journeys, these anomalies disappear because Thessalonians would then have been written prior to the sharpening of the nomistic struggle which climaxed at the conference, and Galatians would have been written shortly after the conference during the third missionary journey. Furthermore, the new hypothesis provides a basis for answering the perplexing problem of the North versus South Galatian theories, allowing one to accept the valid exegetical observations upon which both options have rested. With the mission to North Galatia set prior to the Apostolic Conference, the post-Conference agitation can be placed in A.D. 52, allowing for Galatians to be sent from Ephesus soon after Paul's second visit to North Galatia.

The relationship between the Corinthian letters, Philippians, and Philemon can also be clarified with the new hypothesis. The travel plans announced in Philippians differ from those in Philemon, requiring a separation of the imprisonments reflected in the two letters. There is sufficient time between the Apostolic Conference in 51 and the final Jerusalem journey in 57 to allow for a twenty-seven month Ephesian ministry that concludes with the imprisonment from which Philippians probably was written in the early part of 55. This allows for correlating the plan to visit Macedonia announced in 2 Cor. 1:16 with the plan announced in Phil. 2:19. The Corinthian correspondence can then be placed in the period from spring, 55, through the summer of 56, interrupted by the imprisonment alluded to as the "affliction in Asia" (2 Cor. 1:8) during which Philemon was probably written. There is ample time for this event in the winter of 55-56, followed by a number of months in the summer of 56 during which the missionizing "as far round as Illyricum" (Rom. 15:19) can be placed.

It should perhaps be reiterated in conclusion that the chronological precision allowed by this new hypothesis does not constitute a claim of absolute certainty. Few of the dates and time-spans used here can be verified with high degrees of certainty when taken in isolation. The claim of this theory of chronological interlocking is necessarily modest, namely, that the accommodation with all the ascertainable data has been achieved. The hypothesis is not disproved by the crucial test against the evidence. But a more important criterion can be applied by scholars concerned with historical verification: how well does the hypothesis function as a basis for ascertaining the dates of the Pauline letters and reconstructing the communications between the apostle and his congregations? If the new hypothesis allows others to achieve precise and plausible results in placing such details in their historical sequence, allowing the solution of hitherto insoluble dilemmas,[26] the ultimate purpose of chronological drudgery will have been achieved.

# ABBREVIATIONS

| | |
|---|---|
| *AJT* | American Journal of Theology |
| AnBib | Analecta biblica |
| *ATR* | Anglican Theological Review |
| *BA* | Biblical Archaeologist |
| Bib | Biblica |
| *BJRL* | Bulletin of the John Rylands University Library of Manchester |
| *BLE* | Bulletine de littérature ecclésiastique |
| *BZ* | Biblische Zeitschrift |
| *CAH* | Cambridge Ancient History |
| *CBQ* | Catholic Biblical Quarterly |
| *CJT* | Canadian Journal of Theology |
| *CQR* | Church Quarterly Review |
| *CTM* | Concordia Theological Monthly |
| *DACL* | Dictionnaire d'archéologie chrétienne et de liturgie |
| *DBSup* | Dictionnaire de la Bible, Supplément |
| *DHGE* | Dictionnaire d'histoire et de géographie ecclésiastiques |
| *ET* | Expository Times |
| *EvQ* | Evangelical Quarterly |
| *Exp* | The Expositor |
| *FRLANT* | Forschungen zur Religion und Literatur des Alten und Neuen Testaments |
| *HDB* | Hastings Dictionary of the Bible |
| *HTR* | Harvard Theological Review |
| *HUCA* | Hebrew Union College Annual |
| *IDB* | Interpreter's Dictionary of the Bible |
| *IDBSup* | Supplementary volume to *IDB* |
| *JAAR* | Journal of the American Academy of Religion |

| | |
|---|---|
| *JBL* | Journal of Biblical Literature |
| *JE* | Jewish Encyclopedia |
| *JQR* | Jewish Quarterly Review |
| *JR* | Journal of Religion |
| *JTS* | Journal of Theological Studies |
| *Jud* | Judaica |
| *NCE* | New Catholic Encyclopedia |
| *NKZ* | Neue kirchliche Zeitschrift |
| *NovT* | Novum Testamentum |
| *NTS* | New Testament Studies |
| *PEQ* | Palestine Exploration Quarterly |
| *PG* | Patrologia graeca |
| *PW* | Pauly-Wissowa, Real-Encyclopädie der classischen Altertumswissenschaft |
| *PW*Sup | Supplement to *PW* |
| *RB* | Revue biblique |
| *RE* | Realencyklopädie für protestantische Theologie und Kirche |
| *RevExp* | Review and Expositor |
| *RGG* | Religion in Geschichte und Gegenwart |
| *RHPR* | Revue de l'histoire des philosophie religieuses |
| *RHR* | Revue de l'histoire des religions |
| *RSR* | Revue de science religieuse |
| *SAH* | Sitzungsberichte der Heidelberger Akademie der Wissenschaft, Heidelberg |
| *SK* | Studien und Kritiken |
| *StEv* | Studia Evangelica |
| *StTh* | Studia Theologica |
| *ThQ* | Theologische Quartalschrift |
| *ThR* | Theologische Rundschau |
| *TLZ* | Theologische Literaturzeitung |
| *TU* | Texte und Untersuchungen |
| *TWNT* | Theologisches Wörterbuch zum Neuen Testament, Kittel |
| *TZ* | Theologische Zeitschrift |
| *ZDPV* | Zeitschrift des deutschen Palästina-Vereins |
| *ZNW* | Zeitschrift für die neutestamentliche Wissenschaft |
| *ZThK* | Zeitschrift für Theologie und Kirche |
| *ZWT* | Zeitschrift für wissenschaftlichen Theologie |

# NOTES

## INTRODUCTION

1. Herbert Braun, "Christentum, Entstehung," *RGG*, 3rd ed., I, cols 1685–95; Ferdinand Hahn, *Das Verständnis der Mission im Neuen Testament* (Neukirchen: Neukirchener Verlag, 1963), 76ff.; Ernst Haenchen, *Die Apostelgeschichte* (Göttingen: Vandenhoeck & Ruprecht, 1961, 13th ed.), 60ff.

2. Alfred Suhl, *Paulus und seine Briefe: Ein Beitrag zur paulinischen Chronologie* (Gütersloh: Gerd Mohn, 1975), 314–345.

3. Charles Henry Buck and Greer Taylor, *Saint Paul: A Study in the Development of His Thought* (New York: Scribner, 1969), 214f.

4. John C. Hurd., Jr., "Chronology, Pauline," *IDB Sup*, 167.

5. Gerd Lüdemann, *Paulus der Heidenapostel. I. Studien zur Chronologie* (Göttingen Habilitationsschrift, 1977), 152.

6. Werner Georg Kümmel, *Feine–Behm Einleitung in das neue Testament* (Heidelberg: Quelle & Meyer, 1963, 12th ed.), 179; Willi Marxsen, *Einleitung in das neue Testament: Eine Einführung in ihre Probleme* (Gütersloh: Gerd Mohn, 1963), 25; Donald Guthrie, *New Testament Introduction: The Pauline Epistles* (London: Tyndale, 1961), 278; Wilhelm Michaelis, *Einleitung in das neue Testament* (Bern: Berchtold Haller, 1961, 3rd ed.), 153; Leonhard Goppelt, *The Apostolic and Post-Apostolic Times*, tr. R. A. Guelich (New York: Harper, 1970), 222; Dieter Georgi, *Die Geschichte der Kollekte des Paulus für Jerusalem* (Hamburg–Bergstedt: Reich, 1965), 91–96.

7. John J. Gunther, *Paul: Messenger and Exile: A Study in the Chronology of His Life and Letters* (Valley Forge: Judson, 1972), 13f.

8. Georg Ogg, *The Chronology of the Life of Paul* (London: Epworth, 1968), 200.

9. John A. T. Robinson, *Redating the New Testament* (London: SCM, 1967), 52f.

10. John Knox, *Chapters in a Life of Paul* (New York: Abingdon, 1950), 74ff.

11. M. Jack Suggs, "Concerning the Date of Paul's Macedonian Ministry," *NovT* 4 (1960), 60-68.

12. Robert W. Funk, "The Enigma of the Famine Visit," *JBL* 75 (1956), 130-136; Georg Strecker, "Die sogenannte zweite Jerusalemreise des Paulus," *ZNW* 52 (1962), 67-77.

13. S. Dockx, *Chronologies néotestamentaires et vie de l'Eglise primitive: Recherches exégétiques* (Gembloux: Duculot, 1977).

14. J. R. Richards, "Romans and I Corinthians: Their Chronological Relationship and Comparative Dates," *NTS* 13 (1966-67), 14-30; John C. Hurd, Jr., "The Sequence of Paul's Letters," *CJT* 14 (1968), 189-200; Udo Borse, *Der Standort des Galaterbriefes* (Cologne: Hanstein, 1972), 178.

15. Karl R. Popper, *Conjectures and Refutations: The Growth of Scientific Knowledge* (New York: Harper Torchback, 1968), 15.

16. Carl G. Hempel, *Philosophy of Natural Science* (Englewood Cliffs: Prentice-Hall, 1966), 15.

17. Karl R. Popper, *The Poverty of Historicism* (London: Routledge & Kegan Paul, 1961), 143.

18. W. B. Gallie, "Popper and the Critical Philosophy of History," *The Critical Approach to Science and Philosophy*, ed. M. Bunge (Glencoe: The Free Press, 1964), 410-422; 411.

19. Karl R. Popper, *The Logic of Scientific Discovery* (New York: Harper & Row, 1959), 277.

20. Irving M. Copi, *Introduction to Logic* (New York: Macmillan, 5th ed., 1978).

21. Ibid., 474.

22. Ibid., 476.

23. R. G. Collingwood, "The Historical Imagination," *The Philosophy of History in Our Time: An Anthology Selected, and with an Introduction and Commentary by Hans Meyerhoff* (Garden City: Doubleday and Company, 1959), 64-84; 82.

24. Popper, *Discovery*, 124.

25. Francis Bacon, *The New Organon and Related Writings*, ed. F. H. Anderson (Indianapolis: Bobbs-Merrill, Library of Liberal Arts, 1960), 113.

26. Popper, *Conjectures*, 243.

27. Ibid., 240–245.
28. Popper, *Discovery*, 78, 277.
29. Copi, *Logic*, 478.
30. Ibid., 480.

## CHAPTER I—METHODICAL USE OF THE SOURCES

1. A classic statement of the pro-Lukan apologetic is provided by F. F. Bruce in "Is the Paul of Acts the Real Paul?" *BJRL* 58 (1976), 282–305.

2. See Christoph Burchard, *Der dreizehnte Zeuge. Traditions–und kompositionsgeschichtliche Untersuchungen zu Lukas' Darstellung der Frühzeit des Paulus* (Göttingen: Vandenhoeck & Ruprecht, 1970); W. Ward Gasque, "The Historical Value of the Book of Acts: An Essay in the History of New Testament Criticism," *EvQ* 41 (1969), 68–88; Philipp Vielhauer, "On the 'Paulinism' of Acts," *Studies in Luke–Acts. Essays Presented in Honor of Paul Schubert*, ed. L. E. Keck and J. L. Martyn (New York, Nashville: Abingdon, 1966), 33–50; Hans Conzelmann, *The Theology of St. Luke*, tr. G. Buswell (New York: 1960), and also his article, "Luke's Place in the Development of Early Christianity," *Studies in Luke–Acts*, 298–316; Ernst Haenchen, "The Book of Acts as Source Material for the History of Early Christianity," *Studies in Luke–Acts*, 258–278, and also his section entitled "Lukas als Theologe, Historiker und Schriftsteller," *Apostelgeschichte*, 81–99; Charles Kingsley Barrett, *Luke the Historian in Recent Study* (London: Epworth, 1961). Charles H. Talbert, "An Introduction to Acts," *RevExp* 71 (1974), 437–449, provides a popular introduction to the issues and Erich Grässer, "Acta-Forschung seit 1960," *ThR* 41 (1976), 141–194; 259–290; 42 (1977), 1–68, supplies an exhaustive bibliography. W. Ward Gasque provides a less critical survey of the scholarly discussion since before Baur's time in *A History of the Criticism of the Acts of the Apostles* (Tübingen: Mohr-Siebeck, 1975).

3. The translation of Martin Dibelius' essays on this topic dating from 1923 was done by M. Ling, *Studies in the Acts of the Apostles* (London: SCM, 1956).

4. Cf. W. C. Van Unnick, "Luke–Acts, a Storm Center in Contemporary Scholarship," *Studies in Luke–Acts*, 15–32.

5. Haenchen describes these typical nineteenth century views in *Apostelgeschichte*, 22ff.

6. Cf. Johannes Munck, *The Acts of the Apostles. Introduction, Translation and Notes* (Garden City: Doubleday, 1967), xxxix–xlv.

7. Whether Gasque is willing to undertake this kind of critical evaluation is the question which remains at the end of his otherwise interesting criticism of Haenchen, Conzelmann, et al, in "The Historical Value of the Book of Acts," *EvQ* 41 (1969), 68–88; his *History* published six years later does not fulfill such critical requirements, 276–309.

8. Cf. Arnold Ehrhardt, "The Construction and Purpose of the Acts of the Apostles," *The Framework of the New Testament Stories* (Cambridge: Harvard University Press, 1964), 64ff.; Haenchen, *Apostelgeschichte*, 81ff.; I. Howard Marshall, *Luke: Historian and Theologian* (Exeter: Paternoster Press, 1970), develops this thesis extensively, but I do not share his apologetic harmonizing viewpoint; cf. esp. 69–76; 220–222.

9. Cf. Barrett, *Luke*, 9ff.

10. Cf. Bertil Gärtner, *The Areopagus Speech and Natural Revelation*, tr. C. H. King (Uppsala: Gleerup, 1955); Marshall, *Luke*, 56: "The writings of Luke are plainly indebted to the Old Testament tradition."

11. Hans Conzelmann, *Die Apostelgeschichte* (Tübingen: Mohr-Siebeck, 1963), 9.

12. Cf. Philippe H. Menoud, "Le Plan des Actes des Apôtres," *NTS*, I (1954–55), 47, 51.

13. Cf. Floyd V. Filson, "The Journey-Motif in Luke–Acts," *Apostolic History and the Gospel*, Festschrift F. F. Bruce, ed. W. W. Gasque and R. P. Martin (Grand Rapids: Eerdmans, 1970), 75.

14. Ehrhardt, *Framework*, 90; Helmut Flender, *Heil und Geschichte in der Theologie des Lukas* (Munich: Kaiser, 1965), 98–100, traces this theme through the Gospel and Acts.

15. Burchard offers a successful attempt at this division between traditional materials and redaction in *Zeuge*, 118–124, 150–154, 163–172.

16. Cf. Dibelius, *Studies*, 1ff., and Haenchen, *Apostelgeschichte*, 93ff.

17. Massey Hamilton Shepherd, Jr.'s attempt to revive source criticism to deal with chronological discrepancies between Acts and the epistles was a step in the right direction, but took insufficient account of form and redaction critical insights; "A Venture in the Source Analysis of Acts," *Munera Studiosa: Studies Presented to William Henry Paine Hatch*, ed. M. H. Shepherd, Jr., & S. E. Johnson (Cambridge: Episcopal Theological School, 1946), 91–105. For a more recent attempt in this direction, cf. Jacques Dupont, *Les Sources du Libre des Actes* (Bruges: Desclée de Brouwer, 1960).

18. Cadbury listed the following examples of transitional summaries:

Acts 4:32; 6:7; 9:31; 12:34; 11:23 in "The Summaries in Acts," *The Beginnings of Christianity*, ed. F. J. Foakes–Jackson and K. Lake (London: Macmillan, 1920–33), 5, 392ff. Conzelmann deals with these summaries from a redactional point of view in *Apostelgeschichte*, 7f.

19. Joachim Jeremias, "Untersuchungen zum Quellenproblem des Apostelgeschichte," *ZNW* 36 (1937), 214ff.

20. Cf. Hans Hinrich Wendt, "Die Hauptquellen der Apostelgeschichte," *ZNW* 24 (1925), 293–305.

21. Cf. Adolf von Harnack, "Neue Untersuchungen zur Apostelgeschichte und zur Abfassungszeit der synoptischen Evangelien," *Beiträge zur Einleitung in das Neue Testament* (Leipzig: Hinrichs, 1911), 4, 1–26.

22. Dibelius, *Studies*, 104ff.

23. Ernst Haenchen, "Das Wir in der Apostelgeschichte und das Itinerar," *ZThK* 58 (1961), 362.

24. F. J. Foakes-Jackson and Kirsopp Lake, *The Beginnings of Christianity* (London: Macmillan, 1920–33), 2, 57.

25. Cf. Haenchen, *Apostelgeschichte*, 357.

26. Johannes Weiss, *Über die Absicht und den literarischen Charakter der Apostelgeschichte* (Göttingen: Vandenhoeck & Ruprecht, 1897), 20–40.

27. Haenchen, *ZThK* (1961), 339ff.; Johannes Beutler, "Die paulinische Heidenmission am Vorabend des Apostelkonzils. Zur Redaktionsgeschichte von Apg 14, 1–20," *Theologie und Philosophie* 43 (1968), 360–368, concurs with Haenchen's assessment but does not deal with the crucial differences in theological outlook between these chapters and the rest of Acts.

28. Haenchen, *ZThK* (1961), 345.

29. These details lead E. A. LaVerdiere to develop the "Paul of Antioch" theme in "Paul and the Missions from Antioch," *Bible Today*, 83 (1976), 738–752.

30. Cf. Rudolf Bultmann, "Zur Frage nach den Quellen der Apostelgeschichte," *New Testament Essays in Honor of T. W. Manson*, ed. A. J. B. Higgins (Manchester: University Press, 1959), 78f.

31. Dibelius, *Studies*, 103; Jakob Jervell argues against Dibelius and Haenchen that the period of the early church was not antithetical to the development of written materials concerning the apostles and their activities; "Zur Frage des Traditionsgrundlage der Apostelgeschichte," *StTh* 16 (1962), 25–41.

32. Under the impact of the Qumran discoveries, the notion that an apocalyptically oriented community would not participate in literary activity ought to be finally laid to rest. Cf. CD 1:11ff. for an example of literary polemic written not in spite of but as a consequence of the intense eschatological expectation.

33. Cf. Jeremias, ZNW (1937), 220.

34. Burchard reaches a similar conclusion from his study of the redaction of materials relating to Paul's activities before the missionary expeditions. In comparison with the author's free hand in the shaping of the speeches, the careful citing of historical reminiscences is noted (*Zeuge*, 169); although such details are few, touching mainly on Paul's ". . . person and office as well as his relation to Antioch and particularly to Jerusalem," (171) Burchard concludes it is possible to make a separation between such traditions and the Lukan redaction (172).

35. Haenchen, *Studies in Luke–Acts*, 260.

36. Cf. Henry J. Cadbury, et al, "The Greek and Jewish Traditions of Writing History," *Beginnings*, 2, 7–29; Marshall, *Luke*, 54–57, continues the Cadbury tradition, and Eckhard Plümacher, *Lukas als hellenistischer Schriftsteller: Studien zur Apostelgeschichte* (Göttingen: Vandenhoeck & Ruprecht, 1972), 111–139, provides a balancing perspective.

37. See the positive evaluation of the "we-sections" in Adolf von Harnack, *The Acts of the Apostles*, tr. J. R. Wilkenson (New York: Putnam, 1909), 3ff.

38. Grässer, *ThR* (1976), 188, citing Conzelmann, *Apostelgeschichte*, 5.

39. Cf. DuPont, *Sources*, 73ff. for differing views on this question.

40. Haenchen, *Apostelgeschichte*, 76ff.

41. Philipp Vielhauer, *Geschichte der urchristlichen Literatur: Einleitung in das neue Testament, die Apokryphen und die Apostolischen Väter* (Berlin: de Gruyter, 1965), 391.

42. Eckhard Plümacher, "Wirklichkeitserfahrung und Geschichtsschreibung bei Lukas: Erwägungen zu den Wir-Stücken der Apostelgeschichte," *ZNW* 68 (1977), 2–22; 14.

43. Ibid., 3.

44. Dibelius, *Studies*, 1–25; 123–137.

45. Ibid., 5.

46. Ibid., 6; cf. 125f.

47. Ibid., 5.

48. Ibid., 136.

49. Arthur Darby Nock, *Essays on Religion and the Ancient World* (Cambridge: Harvard University Press, 1972), 2, 821–832.

50. Plümacher, *ZNW* (1977), 5–8; Gottfried Schille, "Die Fragewürdigkeit eines Itinerars der Paulusreisen," *TLZ* 84 (1959), 165–174; cf. also Haenchen, *ZThK* (1961), 329–366.

51. Grässer, *ThR* (1976), 147f.; 190–193.

52. Haenchen, *Apostelgeschichte*, 521; Conzelmann, *Apostelgeschichte*, 116.

53. On similar grounds Munck concluded "there is reason to maintain that the 'we' source goes back to the author of Luke–Acts." *Acts*, xliii.

54. A major argument against the traditional theory that the diarist was identical with the author of Acts is that Acts was written too late for a companion of Paul to still be alive. In fact no one knows when Acts was written except that it must have been some time after A.D. 60 and before 150. Cf. Henry J. Cadbury, *Beginnings* 2, 358: "There is no direct evidence; neither authorship nor date is susceptible of demonstration." The attempts by Conzelmann, *Luke–Acts*, 298–316 and John Knox, "Acts and the Pauline Letter Corpus," *Studies in Luke–Acts*, 279–287, to place Acts in the second century are not convincing. For an example of earlier discussion on this question cf. Johannes de Zwaan, "Was the Book of Acts a Posthumous Edition?" *HTR* 17 (1924), 95–153.

55. Olof Linton, "The Third Aspect. A Neglected Point of View," *StTh* 3 (1950–51), 79–95.

56. Ibid., 82ff.

57. Haenchen reaches a similar conclusion in *Luke–Acts*, 267.

58. Karl Löning offers an excellent model in using redactional, formal, and text critical methods. His study of Acts 9, *Die Saulustradition in der Apostelgeschichte* (Münster: Aschendorff, 1973) traces Luke's redaction of a Saul tradition that had already been edited by a pre–Lukan figure. Unfortunately his study does not touch passages with specific chronological relevance.

59. Paul Billerbeck and H. L. Strack, *Kommentar zum Neuen Testament aus Talmud und Midrasch* (Munich: Beck, 1954, 2d ed.), 2, 747ff.; Haenchen, *Apostelgeschichte*, 481ff.

60. Cf. Foakes-Jackson and Lake, *Beginnings*, 4, 230.

61. Haenchen, *Apostelgeschichte*, 483.

62. This use of "Syria," the technical provincial title for the whole of Palestine including Judea, may be found also in Acts 20:3.

63. Haenchen, *Apostelgeschichte*, 490.

64. Cf. Ernst Käsemann, "Die Johannesjünger in Ephesus," *ZThK* 49 (1952), 144–154.

65. Cf. Haenchen, *Apostelgeschichte*, 504; Ogg, *Chronology*, 135: "The writer of Acts appears to minimize, perhaps he even attempts to conceal, the extent to which the riot was the occasion of Paul's departure from Ephesus."

66. Cf. Conzelmann, *Apostelgeschichte*, 111.

67. Cf. Georgi, *Kollekte*, 84–90; a detailed effort to sustain the Lukan picture in face of critical opinion and the evidence in the Pauline letters can be found in Eduard Herzog, "Die Gefangennehmung des Apostels Paulus in Jerusalem," *Revue International de Théologie*, 13 (1905), 193–224.

68. Haenchen writes, "Die Frage dieser Kollekte und ihrer Aufnahme durch Jerusalem war nichts, was sich ohne grosse Spannung in das lukanische Bild der paulinischen Mission einfügen liess." *ZThK* (1961), 335, note 3. For a less critical view of this issue see Keith F. Nickle, *The Collection. A Study in Paul's Strategy* (London: SCM, 1966); also E. B. Allo, "La portée de la collecte pour Jerusalem dans les plans de saint Paul," *RB* 45 (1936), 529–537.

69. Cf. Conzelmann, *Apostelgeschichte*, 133.

70. Ferdinand Hahn has argued convincingly that the "Apostolic Decree" was worked out by the Jerusalem and Antioch leaders some years after the "Apostolic Conference" which dealt with the question of circumcision. See *Mission*, 70ff. Dibelius, *Studies*, 90, concurs. Representative statements of the traditional view, which retains the Lukan connection between the "Apostolic Decree" and the "Apostolic Conference" of Acts 15, can be found in Benjamin W. Bacon, "The Apostolic Decree Against *Porneia*," *Exp* 7 (1914), 40–61; Idem, "Acts Versus Galatians: The Crux of Apostolic History," *American Journal of Theology* 11 (1907), 467–469. Marcel Simon offers a current version of the same perspective in "The Apostolic Decree and Its Setting in the Ancient Church," *BJRL* 52 (1969–70), 437–460. Daniel Plooij discussed the textual variants in the decree in "The Apostolic Decree and Its Problems," *Exp* 25 (1923), 81–100. For the connections between the decree and late Judaism or early Christianity, cf. A. F. J. Klijn, "The Pseudo–Clementines and the Apostolic Decree," *NovT* 10 (1968), 306–310 and Marc Philonenko, "Le Décret Apostolique et les Interdits Alimentaires du Coran," *RHPR* 43 (1967), 165–172. The study by Jinrich Manek, "Das Aposteldekret im Kontext

der Lukastheologie," *CommViat* 15 (1972), 151–160, tends to confirm the correctness of Hahn's view by showing the role of the decree in the Lukan theory of the gentile mission. Cf. also Traugott Holtz, "Die Bedeutung des Apostelkonzils für Paulus," *NovT* 16 (1974), 124f. William Sanday, "The Apostolic Decree (Acts xv. 20–29)" in *Theologische Studien: Theodor Zahn zum 10 Oktober 1908 dargebracht* (Leipzig: Deichert, 1908), 317–338, was not available.

71. Volker Stolle, *Der Zeuge als Angeklagter: Untersuchungen zum Paulusbild des Lukas* (Stuttgart: Kohlhammer, 1973), 260–284.

72. Ibid., 267.

73. Ibid., 270.

74. Ibid., 275.

75. This in essence is the conclusion reached by Conzelmann about the Gospel of Luke itself, *Luke*, 18ff.

76. This cannot be sidestepped by adducing counter examples in the ancient world in which accounts of journeys were not influenced by redactional manipulation. R. P. C. Hanson's effort to discredit Conzelmann's results overlooks this, "The Journey of Paul and the Journey of Nikias. An Experiment in Comparative Historiography," *StEv*, ed. F. L. Cross (Berlin: Akademie, 1968), 4, 315–318.

77. Cf. Harnack, *Acts*, 6: "It cannot therefore be shown that St. Luke was influenced by a chronological interest in any of the few passages wherein he produces what is practically chronological material from contemporary history. Such a passage as St. Luke iii.1, wherein the chronological situation is scientifically determined, is to be found nowhere in the Acts of the Apostles." There is little evidence therefore in support of C. J. Cadoux's hypothesis that Acts is organized according to a chronological scheme of Pentecost Festivals set every five years; cf. "A Tentative Synthetic Chronology of the Apostolic Age," *JBL* 56 (1937), 177–191.

78. A. N. Sherwin-White, *Roman Society and Roman Law in the New Testament* (Oxford: Clarendon, 1963), 189.

79. Cf. Gasque's discussion in *EvQ* (1969), 68–88; he corrects this impression to a degree in *History*, 277, note 58.

80. Harnack, *Acts*, 22ff.

81. Harnack cannot be accepted on this point; ibid., 19ff.

82. Cf. Vielhauer, *Luke–Acts*, 38–42. For a more positive evaluation of Luke's approach, cf. Günther Bornkamm, "The Missionary Stance of Paul in I Corinthians 9 and in Acts," *Studies in Luke–Acts*, 194–207.

83. Rom. 15:19, 26; 1 Cor. 2:3; 15:8–9; 16:1; 2 Cor. 1:8–10; 4:7–11; 6:4–10; 8:1–5; 9:1–5; 11:9, 22–29, 32–33; 12:2, 14; Gal. 1:13–2:14; 4:12–15; Phil. 1:12–18; 3:4–6; 1 Thess. 1:7–9; 2:2, 17–18; Philem. 1.

84. 1 Cor. 16:8; 2 Cor. 1:1, 23; 2:12–14; 7:5–16; Gal. 1:16–17, 18–19, 21–24; 2:1–10, 11–14; Phil. 4:14–16; 1 Thess. 2:1.

85. Rom. 1:15; 15:23–24, 25, 28; 1 Cor. 4:19; 11:34; 16:3, 5, 8; 2 Cor. 1:15–16; 12:14, 21; 13:1; Phil. 1:27; 2:24; Philem. 22.

86. Rom. 16:21, 22; 1 Cor. 1:11; 16:10, 11, 12, 17, 19; 2 Cor. 1:19; 2:13; 7:5, 13, 14–15; 8:6, 18, 22; 9:5; 12:17–18; Phil. 1:1; 2:19, 25–30; 1 Thess. 1:1; 3:2, 6; 2 Thess. 1:1; Philem. 23–24; Gal. 2:1, 13.

87. For the detailed discussion of the Aretas date, cf. Chapter II.

88. Cf. C. F. Georg Heinrici, *Der zweite Brief an die Korinther* (Göttingen: Vandenhoeck & Ruprecht, 1890), 353ff.

89. For the historical background of the Judaizer attack on Paul, cf. Robert Jewett, "The Agitators and the Galatian Congregation," *NTS* 17 (1970–71), 198–212.

90. Cf. Albrecht Oepke, *Der Brief des Paulus an die Galater* (Berlin: Evangelischer Verlag, 1960), 41ff.; Heinrich Schlier, *Der Brief an die Galater* (Göttingen: Vandenhoeck & Ruprecht, 1962, 12th ed.), 28ff.

91. Jack T. Sanders takes the opposite view in "Paul's 'Autobiographical' Statements in Galatians 1–2," *JBL* 85 (1966), 335–343, suggesting that 1 Cor. 15:1, 3; and 11:23 refute his claim in Gal. 1:11–12 that his gospel was not from men. "Paul forces certain events in his own past to support a particular theological point" (342). These ostensible contradictions are convincing only when one loses sight of Paul's basic argument in each letter. That Paul is independent from the Jerusalem authorities, as argued in Galatians, does not contradict the fact that he had resurrection traditions from the Hellenistic church. Since the truth of Paul's biographical statements in Galatians were sure to be checked by his opponents, it remains highly implausible that he was lying about the degree of his dependence upon the Jerusalem authorities.

CHAPTER II—EXTERNALLY ASCERTAINABLE DATE-RANGES

1. Cf. Joachim Jeremias, "War Paulus Witwer?" *ZNW* 25 (1926), 310–312.

2. Cf. Ogg, *Chronology*, 2–5, citing the critical studies by Erich Fascher, "Zur Witwerschaft des Paulus und der Auslegung von 1 Kor. 7," *ZNW* 28 (1929), 62–69 and Albrecht Oepke, "Probleme der vorchristlichen Zeit des Paulus," *SK* 105 (1933), 387–424; for a more recent discussion of the

problem, see Arlan J. Hultgren, "Paul's Pre–Christian Persecutions of the Church: Their Purpose, Locale, and Nature," *JBL* 95 (1976), 97–111.

3. Gerhard Lohfink does not take this into account in *Paulus vor Damaskus* (Stuttgart: Katholisches Bibelwerk, 1965).

4. Acts 9:11, 30; 11:25; 21:39; 22:3; cf. the basic discussion of the issues in W. C. van Unnik, *Tarsus or Jerusalem. The City of Paul's Youth* (London: Epworth, 1962).

5. Jerome, *Commentary on Philemon*, Migne, *PG* 59, 494, cited by Ogg, *Chronology*, 1–2; cf. also Burchard, *Zeuge*, 34, note 42.

6. Van Unnik, *Tarsus or Jerusalem*, and Joachim Jeremias, "Paulus als Hillelit," *Neotestamentica et Semitica: Studies in Honour of Matthew Black*, ed. E. E. Ellis and M. Wilcox (Edinburgh: T. & T. Clark, 1969), 88–94, accept the traditional view. Morten Enslin, "Paul and Gamaliel," *JR* 7 (1927), 360–375 and Ernst Haenchen, *Apostelgeschichte*, 554, citing Bultmann, raise serious questions that cast doubt on the Gamaliel reference.

7. Cf. the graph of possibilities in Ogg, *Chronology*, 7.

8. Cf. Burchard, *Zeuge*, 27–28.

9. Cf. Ogg, *Chronology*, 11–12; Bihler, J., "Der Stephanusbericht (Apg 6, 8–15 und 7,54–8,2)," *BZ* 3 (1959), 252–270.

10. The study by G. Hölscher, "Die Hohenpriesterliste bei Josephus und die evangelische Chronologie," *SAH*, Phil. –hist. Klasse, 3. Abhandlung (Heidelberg: 1940), mentioned by Lüdemann, *Chronologie*, 280, was not available at the time of final revision. Lüdemann refers on 151 to the "impressive and not fundamentally disproven grounds" set forth by Hölscher for placing the death of Jesus in A.D. 27.

11. August Strobel, "Der Termin des Todes Jesu: Überschau und Lösungsverschlag unter Einschluss des Qumrankalendars," *ZNW* 51 (1960), 69–101; Jack Finegan, *Handbook of Biblical Chronology* (Princeton: Princeton University Press, 1964), 286ff.; Gunther, *Chronology*, 19–24.

12. Joachim Jeremias, *The Eucharistic Words of Jesus*, tr. N. Perrin (New York: Scribners, 1966), 36–41, provides an extensive discussion of the astronomical problem of dating the 15th of Nisan, citing O. Gerhardt, *Der Stern des Messias* (Leipzig–Erlangen: Deichert, 1922), P. V. Neugebauer, *Astronomische Chronologie* (Berlin–Leipzig: de Gruyter, 1929), I, and a number of other works relating to the precise sighting of new light at the beginning of the month. He concludes that Friday, April 7, 30 or Friday, April 3, 33, were both the 14th of Nisan and would fit well with the Johannine chronology. The most recent computerized reckoning of

the astronomical data casts serious doubts on the A.D. 30 option on grounds that Nisan 14 fell on Thursday rather than° Friday that year. Cf. Herman H. Goldstine, *New and Full Moons 1001* B.C. *to* A.D. *1651* (Philadelphia: American Philosophical Society, 1973), 86.

13. Cf. Richard A. Parker and Waldo H. Dubberstein, *Babylonian Chronology 626* B.C.–A.D. *75* (Providence: Brown University Press, 1956); Goldstine, *New and Full Moons*, 86f.

14. Cf. Strobel, ZNW (1960), 81ff.

15. Cf. F. J. Botha, "The Date of the Death of Jesus and the Conversion of Paul," *Ou–Testamentiese Werkemeenskap van Suid–Afrika* (1966), 185.

16. Cf. Eduard Schweizer, *The Lord's Supper According to the New Testament,* tr. J. M. Davis (Philadelphia: Fortress, 1967); the most extensive effort to overcome the discrepancies in the evidence is to be found in Jeremias, *Eucharistic Words,* 41–88.

17. Cf. Eduard Schweizer, *The Good News According to Mark. A Commentary on the Gospel,* tr. D. H. Madvig (London: S.P.C.K., 1971), 294–297; Günther Bornkamm, *Jesus of Nazareth,* tr. I. and F. McLuskey with J. M. Robinson (New York: Harper, 1960), 162: "We may thus assume that the conception of Jesus' Last Supper as the Passover meal goes back to the theology of the first three Evangelists and that of the Christian groups behind them."

18. Cf. H. W. Bartsch, "Die historische Situation des Römerbriefes," *StEv,* ed. F. L. Cross (Berlin: Akademie, 1968), 4, 281–291; Goppelt, *Times,* 79, 81.

19. Gunther, *Chronology,* 19ff.; cf. also Annie Jaubert, *La Date de la Cène: Calendrier Biblique et Liturgie Chrétienne* (Paris: Gabalda, 1957).

20. Luke 4:16–30; August Strobel, "Das apokalyptische Termin-problem in der sogenannten Antrittspredigt Jesu," *TLZ* 92 (1967), 251–254.

21. Cf. Joachim Jeremias, *Jesus' Promise to the Nations* (Naperville: Allenson, 1958); Ben Zion Wacholder suggests Passover, A.D. 28, as the most reasonable date for the start of John the Baptist's ministry, which of course provides a *terminus a quo* for the beginning of Jesus' ministry: "The Calendar of Sabbatical Cycles during the Second Temple and Early Rabbinic Period," *HUCA* 64 (1973), 135–196, esp. 190, and "Sabbatical Chronomessianism and the Timing of Messianic Movements," *HUCA* 66 (1975) 201–218, esp. 215.

22. Cf. Joachim Jeremias, *New Testament Theology: The Proclamation of Jesus,* tr. J. Bowden (New York: Scribners, 1971), 131–141.

23. Cf. Walter Grundmann, *Das Evangelium nach Lukas* (Berlin: Evangelische Verlagsanstalt, n.d.), 123.

24. Cf. Joachim Jeremias, *The Parables of Jesus*, tr. S. H. Hooke (London: SCM, 1963), 119f.; Eta Linnemann, *Jesus of the Parables: Introduction and Exposition*, tr. J. Sturdy (New York: Harper, 1966), 4–47; Robert W. Funk, *Language, Hermeneutic, and Word of God: The Problem of Language in the New Testament and Contemporary Theology* (New York: Harper, 1966) Robert W. Funk and John Dominic Crossan, eds., 124–126; "A Structuralist Approach to the Parables," *Semeia*, I (1974); "The Good Samaritan," *Semeia*, II (1974).

25. Cf. Husband's more plausible suggestion that the 46th year of the temple referred to the traditional period of constructing the second temple of Zerubbabel; citing an article by E. A. Abbott, he shows that the reference in John could not refer to the Herodian temple at all, and thus would have no chronological relevance for the ministry of Jesus; Richard Wellington Husband, "The Year of the Crucifixion," *Transactions of the American Philological Association* 46 (1915), 14–15.

26. Gunther, *Chronology*, 20.

27. Husband, *Transactions*, 21.

28. Friedrich Westberg, *Zur Neutestamentlichen Chronologie und Golgathas Ortslage* (Leipzig: Deichert, 1911), 22–27; J. K. Fotheringham, "The Evidence of Astronomy and Technical Chronology for the Date of the Crucifixion," *JTS* 35 (1934), 146–162; George Ogg, *The Chronology of the Public Ministry of Jesus* (New York: Cambridge University Press, 1940), 244–277; cf. also his article, "The Chronology of the Last Supper," *Historicity and Chronology of the New Testament* ed. D. H. Nineham (London: S.P.C.K. Press, 1965), 92–96; Bo Reicke, *The New Testament Era*, tr. D. E. Green (Philadelphia: Fortress Press, 1968), 183f.; Paul L. Maier, "Sejanus, Pilate, and the Date of the Crucifixion," *Church History* 37 (1968), 3–13; Botha, *Ou–Testamentiese Werkgemeenskap* (1966), 181–190; Husband, *Transactions*, 5–27.

29. Harold W. Hoehner, "Chronological Aspects of the Life of Christ. Part I: The Date of Christ's Birth," *BS* 130 (1973), 338–351.

30. Harold W. Hoehner, "Chronological Aspects of the Life of Christ. Part II: The Commencement of Christ's Ministry," *BS* 131 (1974), 41–54.

31. Harold W. Hoehner, "Chronological Aspects of the Life of Christ. Part III: The Duration of Christ's Ministry," *BS* 131 (1974), 147–162.

32. Harold W. Hoehner, "Chronological Aspects of the Life of Christ. Part IV: The Day of Christ's Crucifixion," *BS* 131 (1974), 241–264. The

problem of the lack of authentic Passover details in the accounts of the Last Supper is not dealt with in this article.

33. Harold W. Hoehner, "Chronological Aspects of the Life of Christ. Part V: The Year of Christ's Crucifixion," *BS* 131 (1974), 332–348.

34. Goldstine, *New and Full Moons*, 87. In contrast, the 15th of Nisan in A.D. 30 apparently fell on Thursday rather than on Friday.

35. Hoehner, "The Year of Christ's Crucifixion," 340.

36. Ibid., 340–347. Husband had suggested in this connection that the "custom" of handing over a prisoner at Passover could only have arisen after A.D. 29, *Transactions*, 8; if this fits in with the ingratiating policies which developed after the execution of Sejanus, it actually could not have commenced before A.D. 32.

37. Philo, *Leg*, 299–305; cf. Paul L. Maier, "The Episode of the Golden Roman Shields in Jerusalem," *HTR* 62 (1969), 109–121; Harold W. Hoehner, *Herod Antipas* (Cambridge: University Press, 1972), 180ff.

38. Charles Kingsley Barrett, *A Commentary on the First Epistle to the Corinthians* (London: Black, 1971, 2nd ed.), 343f.

39. Cf. Johannes Weiss, *Der erste Korintherbrief* (Göttingen: Vandenhoeck & Ruprecht, 1970; repr. of the 9th ed., 1910), 351; Hans Conzelmann, *Der erste Brief an die Korinther* (Göttingen: Vandenhoeck & Ruprecht, 1969), 305.

40. Adolf von Harnack, "Chronologische Berechnung des Tages von Damaskus," *Sitzungsberichte der preussischen Akademie der Wissenschaft zu Berlin*, 37 (1912), 673–682; Westberg, *Chronologie*, 50f., used the same evidence in 1911 to set the conversion of Paul 18 months after the resurrection, i.e., early October, A.D. 34. Westberg's study is not mentioned by Harnack, and it appears the two scholars arrived at their conclusions independently.

41. Irenaeus, Adv. Haer. I, 30;14; 3:2.

42. Cf. Edgar Hennecke, *New Testament Apocrypha*, ed. W. Schneemelcher; tr. R. M. Wilson (Philadelphia: Westminster Press, 1963).

43. Cited from Ogg, *Chronology*, 29.

44. Cf. Henneke, *Apocrypha*, 338; W. C. van Unnik, "The Origin of the Recently Discovered 'Apocryphon Jacobi,'" *Vigiliae Christianae*, 10 (1956), 149–156.

45. Harnack, *Sitzungsberichte* (1912), 679f.; George Ogg concurs in this judgment: "Here then we have a datum that had a place alike in ecclesiastical tradition and in gnostic tradition, and which in consequence

must be very early. It does not owe its existence to metaphysical speculation, and must be rooted in history. . . ." *Chronology*, 29.

46. Cf. for example, the assessment of the Gospel of Thomas materials on the parables of Jesus in Jeremias, *Parables*, 28, 149–151; Wolfgang Schrage, *Das Verhältnis des Thomas–Evangeliums zur synoptischen Tradition und zu den koptischen Evangelienübersetzungen* (Berlin: Töpelmann, 1964).

47. Harnack's suggestion, *Sitzungsberichte*, 678, that the forty days before Jesus' entrance into heavenly rule is a legendary correspondence to the forty days of preparation for his ministry is confirmed by Haenchen, *Apostelgeschichte*, 110–113, and Conzelmann, *Apostelgeschichte*, 21; Philippe H. Menoud argues for the Lukan composition of this datum in "Pendand Quarante Jours," *Neotestamentica et Patristica* (Leiden: Brill, 1962), 148–156.

48. Harnack, *Sitzungsberichte*, 677f.

49. Cf. Suhl, *Chronologie*, 28f.

50. Ibid., 29.

51. Cf. Julius Euting, *Nabatäische Inschriften aus Arabien* (Berlin: Reimer, 1885), 56ff.; Ya'akov Meshorer, *Nabataean Coins* (Jerusalem: Hebrew University Press, 1975; *Qedem: Monographs of the Institute of Archeology*, 3), 41–63; Meshorer provides a useful chart of inscriptions down to the year 39/40 on 46f.

52. W. Schmauch, "Aretas," *RGG*, 3rd ed. I, col. 590.

53. Emil Schürer, *Geschichte des jüdischen Volkes im Zeitalter Jesu Christi* (Leipzig: Hinrich, 1901–1909, 4th ed.), I, 736ff.; Stewart Perowne, *The Later Herods. The Political Background of the New Testament* (London: Hodder & Stoughton, 1958), 202; A. Negev, "The Chronology of the Middle Nabatean Period," *PEQ* 101 (1969), 5.

54. A. von Gutschmid, "Verzeichniss der nabatäischen Könige," *Nabatäische Inschriften aus Arabien*, ed. J. Euting (Berlin: Reimer, 1885), 84–89; *PW* 2, col. 674; A. Plummer, *A Critical and Exegetical Commentary on the Second Epistle of St. Paul to the Corinthians* (Edinburgh: Clark, 1915), 333.

55. Lake, *Beginnings*, 5, 193.

56. Haenchen, *Studies in Luke–Acts*, 268ff.

57. Carl Watzinger described the layout of the gates and towers as discovered by intensive surface examination, *Damaskus, die antike Stadt* (Berlin: Gruyter, 1921), 60ff.; A. von Kremer described the broad sur-

rounding oasis in *Topographie von Damascus, Denkschriften der Kaiserlichen Akademie der Wissenschaften* (Phil.-hist. Classe; Vienna, 1854–55), 5, 1–7; map opposite 36.

58. F. M. Abel, *Géographie de la Palestine* (Paris: Gabalda, 1938), 2, 141ff.

59. Ibid., 142ff.; H. Bietenhard, "Die Dekapolis von Pompeius bis Trajan. Ein Kapital aus der neutestamentliche Zeitgeschichte," *ZDPV* 79 (1963), 24–58.

60. Schürer, *Geschichte*, 2, 94ff.

61. Ibid., 150ff.; Paul Ewald, "Aretas," *RE* 1, 795–797; R. Janin, "Damas," *DHGE* 14, 42–47; H. Leclercq, "Paul (Saint)," *DACL* 13, 2579; Abel, *Géographie*, 2, 301f.; Bietenhard, *ZDPV* (1963), 25–68; Alphons Steinmann, *Aretas IV. König der Nabatäer. Eine historisch–exegetische Studie zu 2 Kor 11,32f.*, (Freiburg: Herder, 1909), 33–37; Ernst Barnikol, "War Damaskus um 37 n. Chr. arabisch? 2. Kor 11,32–33 und Gal 1,17," *Theologische Jahrbücher*, 1 (1933), 93–95.

62. Emil Schürer, "Der Ethnarch des Königs Aretas," *Theologische Studien und Kritiken*, 72 (1899), 95–99.

63. Several recent studies have concluded that it is simply not possible to discover when Aretas IV controlled Damascus. John Irving Lawlor, *The Nabataeans in Historical Perspective* (Grand Rapids: Baker, 1974), 188, cites agreement with the statement of Jean Starcky, "The Nabataeans: A Historical Sketch," *BA* 18 (1955), 98: "The question remains open."

64. Schürer notes in *Geschichte*, 2, 153f., that even during Tiberius' era Damascus was involved in a border strife with Sidon which indicates the Damascene territory joined directly onto the Sidonian border, far to the west.

65. Ibid., 152.

66. Abel, *Géographie*, 2, 145.

67. Cf. S. A. Cook, M. P. Charlesworth, S. P. Adcock, eds., *The Cambridge Ancient History* (Cambridge: University Press, 1928; rep. of the 1924 ed.), 10, 744ff.

68. Cf. Perowne, *Later Herods*, 57.

69. Cf. Ogg, *Chronology*, 22.

70. Cf. Schürer, *Geschichte*, 1, 459.

71. The lack of coins is frequently asserted; cf. Leclercq, *DACL* 13, 2579; *PW* 2, col 674. But the sole evidence seems to be Théodore Edme Mionnet's listing of coins found up until the early nineteenth century,

*Description de Médailles antiques, Grecques et Romaines* (Paris: Festu, 1806–1813), 5, 284–292. Since Mionnet lists only five coins found in Damascus during Tiberius' reign and three during Nero's, this can scarcely be viewed as an exhaustive sampling.

72. Cf. *CAH* 10, 660; Hugo Willrich, "Caligula," *Klio*, 3 (1903), 302f.

73. Thomas Spencer Jerome's analysis of the Caligula administration lends some credence to this assertion that the transfer took place in the early years. He notes that the emperor's enthusiasm for anti–Tiberius policies waned half–way through his reign as he discovered the complicity of the Senate in the plot against his family. He then began to speak favorably of Tiberius and unfavorably of the Senate. *Aspects of the Study of Roman History* (New York: Putnam, 1923), 410ff.

74. J. P. V. D. Balsdon, *The Emperor Gaius* (Oxford: Clarendon, 1934), 197.

75. "Die Geschichte der Nabatäer," *Petra und das Königreich der Nabatäer: Lebensraum, Geschichte und Kultur eines arabischen Volkes der Antike,* ed. M. Lindner (Munich: Delp, 1974, 2d ed.), 130f.

76. Cf. C. H. Turner, "Chronology of the New Testament," *HDB* 1, 416f.; Steinmann's study, *Aretas IV,* 43, comes to essentially the same conclusion, setting the *terminus a quo* in A.D. 37 and the *terminus ad quem* in 40.

77. Cf. Eduard Schwartz, *Gesammelte Schriften,* 5, 124–169; also "Noch Einmal der Tod der Söhne Zebedai," *ZNW* 11 (1910), 89–104; S. Safrai and M. Stern, eds., *The Jewish People in the First Century* (Philadelphia: Fortress, 1974), 1, 299; for an opposing view cf. Lake, *Beginnings,* 5, 445–452.

78. Gunther, *Chronology,* 36–44; Hahn, *Mission,* 76ff.; Suhl, *Chronologie,* 315–321.

79. Schwartz, *Gesammelte Schriften,* 5, 124–169: the essay first appeared in 1907.

80. Ibid., 129.

81. Gerhardt Delling correctly concludes that the evidence speaks strongly against James and John having suffered death at the same time; see "Johannes, der Apostel," *RGG,* 3rd ed., 3, col 803. Karl Heussi attempts to ward off criticisms of the martyrdom hypothesis, placing the execution of James and John in the spring of A.D. 44, following an Apostolic Conference, in "Petrus und die beiden Jakobus in Galater 1–2," *Wissenschaftliche Zeitschrift Jena,* 6 (1956–57), 147–152. Eduard Schwartz provides an exhaustive discussion of the patristic evidence in

"Über den Tod der Söhne Zebedaei: Ein Beitrag zur Geschichte des Johannesevangeliums," *Gesammelte Schriften*, 5 (Berlin: de Gruyter, 1963), 48–123.

82. Cf. Lake, *Beginnings*, 5, 452; G. B. Caird, "Chronology of the NT," *IDB* 1, 603f.; Daniel Plooij, *De Chronologie van het Leven van Paulus* (Leiden: Brill, 1918), 15, places the date of the 15th of Nisan on April 1, A.D. 44.

83. Joachim Jeremias, "Sabbathjahr und neutestamentliche Chronologie," *ZNW* 27 (1928), 98–103.

84. Robert W. Funk, "The Enigma of the Famine Visit," *JBL* 75 (1956), 130–136.

85. In fact the pressure of the seventeen year span at the beginning of Paul's ministry inserts a distorting element into the dating of the famine itself; Jeremias' argument for dating the famine in 47–48, necessitated by the coordination with Pauline chronology in his hypothesis, actually rests on sheer probability that there was a famine during a sabbath year. A further difficulty is that the sabbatical year fell not in 47–48 but in 48–49, according to the reliable recent study by Ben Zion Wacholder, *HUCA* (1973), 191. There is in fact no direct evidence that either the famine or the relief mission took place at that time. Leclercq notes in contrast that Helen of Adiabene visited Jerusalem with relief supplies during the years 44–45, which would indicate the famine began considerably before the date Jeremias suggested, *DACL* 13, 2568–2699. Kenneth S. Gapp, "The Universal Famine under Claudius," *HTR* 28 (1935), 258–265, infers the presence of a famine from the fall of A.D. 44 to the spring of 46 because of the unusually high grain prices in Egypt. There is conflicting evidence on this question in Josephus, *Ant.*, XX, 101. But the difficulty of setting a precise date on the basis of probability alone is evidently not seen by those who have accepted Jeremias' date. See, for example, Nickle, *Collection*, 31f.

86. Cf. Ernst Bammel, "Judenverfolgung und Naherwartung. Zur Eschatologie des Ersten Thessalonicherbriefes," *ZThK* 56 (1959), 294–315.

87. Buck and Taylor, *Saint Paul*, 148.

88. Cf. Bammel, *ZThK* (1959), 295, 306.

89. Cf. Robert Jewett, "The Agitators and the Galatian Congregation," *NTS* 17 (1970–71), 205, note 5.

90. Cf. Ernest Best, *A Commentary on the First and Second Epistles to the Thessalonians* (London: Adam & Charles Black, 1972), 120.

91. Buck and Taylor, *St. Paul*, 150–162.

92. Ibid., 158.

93. Cf. Best, *Thessalonians*, 5.

94. Buck and Taylor, *St. Paul*, 161f.

95. Ibid., 162.

96. Cf. the accounts of the debate in Josef Ernst, *Die eschatologischen Gegenspieler in den Schriften des Neuen Testaments* (Regensburg: Pustet, 1967); Charles H. Giblin, *The Threat to Faith. An Exegetical and Theological Re-examination of 2 Thessalonians 2* (Rome: Pontifical Biblical Institute, 1967); Ernst Best, *Thessalonians*; and J. Schmid, "Der Antichrist und die hemmende Macht," *ThQ* 129 (1949), 323–343.

97. Wilhelm Bousset, *The Anti-Christ Legend*, tr. A. H. Keane (London: Hutchinson, 1896), 136ff.

98. Giblin, *Thessalonians*, 66ff.

99. Best, *Thessalonians*, 284.

100. F. Mussner, "Das Buch Judith und die neutestamentliche Antichristidee," *Trier Theologische Zeitschrift* 72 (1963), 243.

101. Otto Betz, "Der Katechon," *NTS* 9 (1962–63), 277.

102. Best, *Thessalonians*, 288; Betz, NTS (1962–63), argues in contrast that the background of Daniel 9:24ff. points toward a Roman emperor as the restrainer.

103. Cf. Bousset, *Anti–Christ*.

104. Oscar Cullmann, "Le charactère eschatologique du devoir missionaire et de la conscience apostolique de S. Paul," *RHPR* 16 (1936), 210–245.

105. Johannes Munck, *Paul and the Salvation of Mankind*, tr. F. Clark (London: SCM, 1959), 36–42.

106. J. E. Frame, *A Critical and Exegetical Commentary on the Epistles of St. Paul to the Thessalonians* (Edinburgh: Clark, 1912), 261f.

107. Giblin, *Thessalonians*, 167ff.; D. W. Robinson, "II Thess. 2:6, 'That which restrains,' or 'That which holds sway'?" *StEv* 2, 635–638.

108. August Strobel, *Untersuchungen zum eschatologischen Verzögerungsproblem* (Leiden: Brill, 1961), 98–116; Ernst, *Gegenspieler*, 55ff.; this position is convincingly argued by Roger D. Aus, "God's Plan and God's Power: Isaiah 66 and the Restraining Factors of 2 Thess 2:6–7," *JBL* 96 (1977), 537–553.

109. Cf. Wayne A. Meeks, ed., *The Writings of St. Paul* (New York: Norton, 1972), 111, note 7 comments on the interpretation of 2 Thess. 2:6: "If the original readers 'know,' as Paul says, the puzzling force or person who holds back the events of the end, the secret died with them,

for subsequent commentators have conjectured every possible identification. . . ."

110. Cf. Ogg, *Chronology*, 60–65 for the text of this and other related
inscriptions.

111. Cf. Ogg, ibid., 63; also Lake, *Beginnings* 5, 455ff. and *PW* 2-A,
2, cols 1715–1719.

112. Merrill F. Unger, "Archeology and Paul's Tour of Cyprus," *BS* 117
(1960), 233, seems to imply that a more precise chronological inference
is possible from this inscription, but he fails to provide an adequate discussion of the issues.

113. Cf. William M. Ramsay, "The Family and Religion of L. Sergius
Paullus, Proconsul of Cyprus," *ET* 29 (1917–18), 324–328; William M.
Calder, "A Galatian Estate of the Sergii Paulli," *Klio* 24 (1930–31), 59–62;
*PW* 2-A, 2, col 1718; for a conflicting view see Theodor Zahn, *Introduc-
tion to the New Testament*, tr. directed by M. W. Jacobus (New York:
Scribners, 1917, 2nd ed.), 3, 463ff.

114. W. Seston deals with much of this literature prior to 1931 in
"L'Empereur Claude et les Chrétiens," *RHPR* 11 (1931), 275–304; more
recent literature is dealt with by Ogg, *Chronology*, 99–103 and Stephen
Benko, "The Edict of Claudius of A.D. 49 and the Instigator Chrestus,"
*TZ* 25 (1969), 406–418.

115. Arnaldo Momigliano, *Claudius. The Emperor and His Achievement*, tr. W. D. Hogarth (Oxford: Clarendon, 1934), 20ff.

116. Some scholars have erroneously concluded that Suetonius' reference was to this edict in the year 41, but Dio Cassius explicitly states that
the Jews were not expelled at this early date. H. Janne does not take this
into account in "Impulsore Chresto," *Annuaire de l'Institut de Philologie
et d'Histoire Orientales et Slaves*, 2 (1934–35), 531–535; 4 (1936), 275–
293. For background on the legal status of Jews in Rome and their experience in an earlier banning, cf. Elmer Truesdell Merrill, "The Expulsion of
Jews from Rome under Tiberius," *Classical Philology* 14 (1919), 365–372.

117. E. Mary Smallwood writes in *The Jews Under Roman Rule*
(Leiden: Brill, 1976), 211: "The only reasonable interpretation of Suetonius' sentence is that the reference is to Christianity, though he was
apparently under the misapprehension that 'Chrestus' was a rabble-rouser
present in person." After a detailed discussion, she accepts the Orosius
date of A.D. 49 for the expulsion, (215); only Christian agitators were
affected, (216). Cf. Robert O. Hoerber, "The Decree of Claudius in Acts

18:2," *CTM* 31 (1960), 690: ". . . we may assume that heated discussions in the Jewish community at Rome concerned the acceptance of Jesus as the Christ, and we may conjecture that Suetonius, misinterpreting his source, as he seems to do not infrequently, thought Christus (or Chrestus, as the name was often spelled, with the pronunciation no doubt being the same in the Greek of the day) was present in person to stir up trouble." Benko's effort to show that Chrestus was a Jew who became an enemy of his Hellenistic Roman neighbors and thus caused the riot is less plausible than the consensus summarized by Hoerber; *TZ* (1969), 406–418.

118. Vincent M. Scramuzza, *The Emperor Claudius* (Cambridge: Harvard University Press, 1940), 151. Marcus Borg suggests in "A New Context for Romans 13," *NTS* 19 (1972–73), 212f. that nationalistic agitation within the Roman synagogues provides the background for Claudius' action. He agrees that "Chrestus" means "Christus," or messiah, referring to Tertullian's comment in Apol. 3 that Roman emperors tended to pronounce the *i* of *christianus* as an *e*. But he finds it more plausible to believe that messianic agitation unrelated to early Christianity was in view. Why this should have caused the expulsion of Christians like Aquila and Priscilla is unanswerable with Borg's hypothesis.

119. Hoerber, *CTM* 31 (1960), 692–694, cites Acts 2:5; 3:18; 8:1; 9:35; 19:10; Matt. 3:5–6; Mark 1:36–37; John 3:26; he shows that the predicate position of *pantes* in Acts 18:2 does not imply totality and allows the interpretation "that only the 'ringleaders' suffered banishment." The expulsion of the entire Jewish population in Rome, estimated at around 50,000, would have been too massive an undertaking to have been overlooked by Roman historians. Haenchen, *Apostelgeschichte*, 475, concurs with the conclusion that only the agitators were banished.

120. *Seven Books of History Against the Pagans. The Apology of Paulus Orosius*, tr. J. W. Raymond (New York: Columbia University Press, 1936), 302; i.e., *History*, 7, 6, 15.

121. Cf. Leclercq, *DACL* 13, 2610.

122. Cf. Ogg, *Chronology*, 102f.

123. Harnack, *Sitzungsberichte* (1912), 675f.

124. Cf. Caird, *IDB* 1, 604.

125. Cf. Ogg, *Chronology*, 103: "The fact that the date given by Orosius thus harmonizes so satisfactorily with Acts cannot be taken without more ado as proof of its soundness; but it is certainly remarkable."

126. Cf. Lake, *Beginnings*, 5, 459; Scramuzza, *Claudius*, 287; Momigli-

ano, *Claudius*, 37. Harry J. Leon, *The Jews of Ancient Rome* (Philadelphia: Jewish Publication Society, 1960), agrees with this reconstruction of the events but refuses to place reliance on Orosius' date.

127. Cf. Lake, *Beginnings*, 5, 464; Finegan, *Chronology* 319; W. Rees, "Gallio the Proconsul of Achaia (Acts 18:12–17)," *Scripture. The Quarterly of the Catholic Biblical Association*, 4 (1949–51), 11–20; B. Schwank, "Der sogenannte Brief an Gallio und die Datierung des 1 Thess," *BZ* 15 (1971), 265–266.

128. Hans Hinrich Wendt, *Die Apostelgeschichte* (Göttingen: Vandenhoeck & Ruprecht, 1913, 9th ed.), 60; W. Larfeld, "Die delphische Gallioinschrift und die paulinische Chronologie," *NKZ* 34 (1923), 644, concurs.

129. K. Haacker, "Die Gallio–Episode und die paulinische Chronologie," *BZ* 16 (1972), 254f.

130. Karl Georg Wieseler, *Chronologie des apostolischen Zeitalters* (Göttingen: Vandenhoeck & Ruprecht, 1848), 119ff.

131. Adolf Deissmann, *Paul. A Study in Social and Religious History*, tr. W. E. Wilson (London: Hodder & Stoughton, 1926), 264, refers to the study by H. Lehmann written in 1858.

132. Cf. Rees, *Scripture*, 16.

133. For a history of the publication and early translation of this inscription from Delphi see Deissmann, *Paul*, 261ff.

134. Cf. André Plassart, "L'inscription de Delphes mentionnant le Proconsul Gallion," *Revue d'études grecques* 80 (1967), 377.

135. Deissmann, *Paul*, 281.

136. Kirsopp Lake, *Beginnings*, 5, 460ff.; Haenchen, *Apostelgeschichte*, 58ff.; Leclercq, *DACL* 13, 2612: "between April and the 1st of August in 52;" Ogg, *Chronology*, 110: "at some time in the first half of A.D. 52." Luigi Cantarelli, "Gallione proconsole di Acaia e S. Paolo," *Rendiconti della R. Accademia Nazionale dei Lincein, Classe de Scienze Morali, Storiche e Filologiche*, Serie 5, 32 (1923), 166: "January–August, 52."

137. A. Brassac, "Une inscription de Delphes et la chronologie de Saint Paul," *RB* 22 (1913), 36–53; 207–217, provides a photograph by E. Bourguet of the additional fragments of the inscription taken in 1910; cf. Plassart, *Revue de études grecques* (1967), 375, for a reference to two small fragments beyond those discussed by Brassac.

138. J. H. Oliver reviews Plassart's restoration of the somewhat mangled inscription, and argues that the suggestion of *eia se* in line 17 is less likely than *entellomai hymein*, which means that Deissmann had been right in

supposing the epistle was addressed to the city of Delphi or the Amphytionic Council while Gallio was still proconsul; "The Epistle of Claudius Which Mentions the Proconsul Junius Gallio," *Hesperia* 40 (1971), 239f.

139. Brassac, *RB* (1913), 378; he places the letter in the first weeks of spring, A.D. 52; 49f.

140. Cf. Dio Cassius, LVII, 14, 5.

141. Theodor Mommsen, *Römisches Staatsrecht* (Graz: Akademische Druck, 1952, 2nd ed.), 2, 256; Larfeld, *NKZ* (1923), 638; cf. also Caird, *IDB* 1, 604; Finegan, *Chronology*, 316, argues in contrast for accession in May or June in A.D. 51.

142. Haenchen, *Apostelgeschichte*, 59; Gunther, *Chronology*, 172, note 1, overlooks this important consideration in dating the accession to office in May, 52 and Paul's hearing in May, June, or July, 52.

143. Mommsen, *Staatsrecht*, 1, 255.

144. Deissmann, *Paul*, 279.

145. E. Groag, *Die römischen Reichsbeampten von Achaia bis auf Diocletian* (Vienna: Hoelder–Pichler–Temsky, 1939), 32–35, likewise sets Gallio's term in the years 51–52.

146. Although *Bell.* II, 261–263 states that the Egyptian had 30,000 followers, the more sober account in *Ant.* XX, 167–172, noting that 400 were slain and 299 taken prisoner, seems to indicate a force more nearly the size reported by Acts. Lake suggests in *Beginnings*, 4, 277, that a textual corruption in Josephus from $\triangle$ ( =4) to $\wedge$ ( =30) may account for the discrepancy. At any rate the figure of 4000 is more probable.

147. Cf. Plooij, *Chronologie*, 68ff.

148. Cf. Ogg, *Chronology*, 163: ". . . there need be no doubt that the events recorded in Josephus *Ant.* XX, 160–81 . . . took place onwards from the end of A.D. 55 and that, while there may be some overlapping, the order in which these events are given is chronological."

149. Wacholder, *HUCA* (1975), 216.

150. Sherwin-White, *Roman Society*, 68.

151. Haenchen, *Apostelgeschichte*, 61.

152. This date fits in well with Josephus' comment that Felix was sent to Palestine before Agrippa's promotion which took place in Claudius' twelfth year. Lake concludes from this evidence that Felix ". . . probably was sent to Palestine in 52 or possibly in 53." *Beginnings*, 5, 464.

153. Ibid., 464ff., Haenchen, *Apostelgeschichte*, 60ff.; Conzelmann, *Apostelgeschichte*, 130; Kümmel, *Einleitung*, 177.

154. Robert H. Pfeiffer, *History of New Testament Times* (New York:

Harper, 1949), 39; Schürer, *Geschichte*, 1, 579ff.; Bury, Cook, and Adcock, ed., *CAH* 10, 854; Martin Hengel, *Die Zeloten. Untersuchungen zur jüdischen Freiheitsbewegung in der Zeit von Herodes I. bis 70 n. Chr.* (Leiden: Brill, 1961), 359, note 4; Perowne, *Later Herods*, 101; Safrai and Stern, ed., *Jewish People*, 76; Smallwood provides a tenure for Felix of 6–7 years, from A.D. 52–58/9, *Roman Rule*, 269.

155. Josephus, *Bell.* II, 284; cf. Schürer, *Geschichte*, 1, 587.

156. Festus died sometime before Albinus took office, leaving a period of leaderless anarchy (Josephus, *Ant.* XX, 197–203; cf. *PW* 22, 1, cols 221f.

157. Plooij, *Chronologie*, 70.

158. Adolph von Harnack, *Die Chronologie des altchristlichen Litteratur bis Eusebius* (Leipzig: Hinrichs, 1897), 1, 238.

159. Cook, Charlesworth, and Adcock, *CAH* 10, 709; Caird disagrees at this point but concurs that Pallas' influence was as great after his dismissal as before; *IDB* 1, 604.

160. Cf. Plooij, *Chronologie*, 68; Ramsay also argued that Pallas had sufficient power to help his brother after the year 55; see "Pauline Chronology," *Exp*, 5th Series, 5 (1897), 210; Schürer, *Geschichte*, 1, 578, agrees. His view is developed in detail in "Zur Chronologie des Lebens Pauli, zugleich ein Beitrag zur Kritik der Chronik des Eusebius," *ZWT* 41 (1898), 21–42, esp. 39f.

161. For a detailed discussion of the Eusebius datum, cf. Ogg, *Chronology*, 151–155.

162. An argument to this effect may be found in *PW*, 22, 1, cols 224f.

163. Johannes Weiss, *Earliest Christianity. A History of the Period* A.D. *30–150* (New York: Harper, 1959), tr. F. C. Grant et al, 1, 377, note 115.

164. Cf. Schürer, *Geschichte*, 1, 579: "at the earliest 58, the latest 61, probably 60." Among the more recent scholars who agree on the date of 60 are Erich Fascher, "Paulus (Apostel)," *PWSup* 8, col 453; Perowne, *Later Herods*, 101.

165. Plooij decides for 59, although there are some mistakes in his argument; *Chronologie*, 58ff. Caird decided for 59 in *IDB* 1, 604f. as did Leclercq in *DACL* 13, 2643. William Mitchell Ramsay strongly supported this date in *Pauline and Other Studies in Early Christian History* (London: Hodder & Stoughton, 1906), 345ff.

166. Safrai and Stern, eds., *Jewish People*, 76, cites in this connection Ya'akov Meshorer, *Jewish Coins of the Second Temple Period* (Tel Aviv: Am Hassefer, 1967), 103.

167. Cf. Schürer, *Geschichte*, 2, 272.

168. Perowne, *Later Herods*, 98; Conzelmann, *Apostelgeschichte*, 127.

169. Cf. Schürer, *Geschichte*, 2, 272; R. Schmidt, "Ananias," *RE*, 1, 488; A. Büchler, "Ananias, Son of Nebedeus," *JE*, 1, 558–559. Westberg, *Chronologie*, 56, concludes that Ananias is the Eleazar ben Chaisan mentioned in b. Joma 9a in the Talmud as having served 10 years as high priest, i.e., from A.D. 47–57. He argues further that Ananias' successor could not have started earlier than 56, and that the transition must have been close to the time Felix was recalled, since both events are mentioned in conjunction by Josephus, *Ant.* XX, 8,8.

170. Wieseler, *Chronologie*, 83; Plooij, *Chronologie*, 81–83.

171. Carl Clemen, *Paulus. Sein Leben und Wirken* (Giessen: Töpelmann, 1904), 1, 386.

172. Cf. Ogg, *Chronology*, 176: "To infer from the singular . . . in the Western text that Paul's arrival in Rome must be dated earlier than A.D. 62 is, however, extremely precarious." Ogg, 177, goes on to discuss the scholarly debate concerning the Latin translation of Acts 28:16; Eugene Dabrowski summarizes scholarly opinion in "Le Prétendu Procès Romain de S. Paul D'Après les Recherches Récentes," AnBib, 2 (1961), 203, but does not touch on the chronological implications.

173. Bauer lists advocates and opponents of the Spanish mission hypothesis in *Lexicon*, 786, and the dividing line is marked by scholarly attitudes about the authenticity of the Pastorals.

174. Cf. Ogg, *Chronology*, 178–200; Gunther, *Chronology*, 139–150; other key studies are F. Pfister, "Die zweimalige römische Gefangenschaft und die spanische Reise des Apostels Paulus und der Schluss der Apostelgeschichte," ZNW 14 (1913): 216–221 and M. Meinertz, "Worauf bezeiht sich die *prōtē apologia?*" *Bib*, 4 (1923): 390–394.

175. Cf. Ogg, *Chronology*, 192–198 and Pfister, ZNW (1913), 216–221; for a discussion of the Acts of Peter, cf. Hennecke–Schneemelcher, *Apocrypha*, 2, 177–221.

176. Goppelt, *Times*, 104, writes "The Canon Muratori, which was the first to maintain a visit to Spain, probably came to this conclusion on the basis of Rom. xv and I Clem. v, since we have no other direct tradition for such a visit." Cf. Albert C. Sundberg, Jr., "Muratorian Fragment," *IDB Sup*, 609–610 for the evidence of fourth century provenance of this writing.

177. J. N. Hillgarth, "Spain. I. Early," *NCE* 13, 494–496. The most extensive study of Spanish church history, P. P. Gams, *Die Kirchengeschichte von Spanien* (Regensburg: 1862–79; repr. in Graz: 1956), docu-

ments this conclusion in detail. W. P. Bowers refutes the frequently stated view that Paul would have missionized in the synagogues there. In "Jewish Communities in Spain in the Time of Paul the Apostle," *JTS* 26 (1975), 375–402; 400, he writes "That there were Jewish communities in Spain prior to this (A.D. 70–135) is not supported by any evidence currently available."

178. Cf. Ogg, *Chronology*, 189–191; Donald Alfred Hagner, *The Use of the Old and New Testaments in Clement of Rome* (Leiden: E. J. Brill, 1973), 220; Karlmann Beyschlag, *Clemens Romanus und der Frühkatholizismus* (Tübingen: Mohr/Siebeck, 1966), 267–299, shows that Clement's picture of Paul is decisively shaped by the world mission conception of Judaism, consistent with the early Catholic theology of Luke–Acts. Beyschlag denies that 1 Clem. 5: 7 relates to the presumed Spanish mission of Paul, 298; cf. also 32, note 6. An earlier study of the problem is E. Dubowy, *Klemens von Rom über die Reise Pauli nach Spanien* (Freiburg: Herder, 1914).

179. For a discussion of the relation between the persecution and the date of the fire, cf. M. J. Costelloe, "Nero, Roman Emperor," *NCE* 10, 341–342.

180. Cf. Haenchen, *Apostelgeschichte*, 650–656; Dabrowski, AnBib (1961), 197–207, provides a skeptical evaluation of the efforts to build a case for Paul's release on legal grounds. Key views on this point are Kirsopp Lake, "What Was the End of St. Paul's Trial?" *Interpreter*, 5 (1909), 146–156, and L. P. Pherigo, "Paul's Life After the Close of Acts," *JBL* 70 (1951), 277–284.

181. Cf. Conzelmann, *Apostelgeschichte*, 150; Haenchen, *Apostelgeschichte*, 656. Hans Lietzmann rejected earlier forms of the argument that the author of Acts intentionally refrained from recounting Paul's execution, but Schwartz and others whom he tries to refute did not have access to redactional critical techniques that lend such plausibility to the Haenchen–Conzelmann consensus; cf. *Petrus und Paulus in Rome* (Bonn: Marcus & Weber, 1915), 238–252. The definitive recent statement of the redaction critical conclusion is in Hans–Joachim Michel, *Die Abschiedsrede des Paulus an die Kirche Apg 20,17–38: Motivegeschichte und theologische Bedeutung* (Munich: Kösel, 1973), 77.

182. F. Schroeder, "Paul, Apostle, St.," *NCE* 11, 1–11; 7f. Carl Erbes, "Die Todestage der Apostel Paulus und Petrus," *TU* 19, Heft 1 (1899), 1–138, argues for placing the date of Paul's execution after a two year imprisonment commencing on Feb. 12, 61; the execution date of Feb. 22,

63, correlates with the fourth century festival of the martyrdom of St. Paul, 40–55.

183. Arnaldo Momigliano, "Nero," *CAH*, 10, 720; Will Durant, *Caesar and Christ* (New York: Simon and Schuster, 1944), 279, explicitly states that "The law of *maiestas* was revived" in A.D. 62 and implies that Seneca's dismissal was related to his protests.

184. Hohl, "Domitius (Nero)," *PWSup* 3 (1918), 349–394, esp. 374ff. provides a detailed reconstruction of the events in the first six months of A.D. 62.

185. Cf. Dabrowski, AnBib (1961), 201; Haenchen, *Apostelgeschichte*, 593.

186. Cf. Theodor Mommsen, "Die Rechtsverhältnisse des Apostels Paulus," *ZNW* 2 (1901), 81–96; Hans Lietzmann, "Ein neuer Fund zur Chronologie des Paulus," *Zeitschrift für wissenschaftliche Theologie*, n.f., 18 (1911), 345–354; Henry J. Cadbury, "Roman Law and the Trial of Paul," *Beginnings*, 5, 297–338. It is not necessary to assume a normal trial was required in the treason hysteria of A.D. 62; Philipp reports in *PW*, Series 2, 1, Part 1 (1914), 1160–61 that Rubellius Plautus was summarily beheaded by the centurion without any previous legal process.

187. Cf. Lea Roth, "Poppaea, Sabina," *EJ* 13, 861. This assessment is confirmed by Rudolf Hanslik, "Poppaea Sabina," *PW* 22, Part 1 (1953), 85–91; esp. 87f. which discusses the Jewish persons Poppaea was able to assist and suggests this was a factor in the persecution of Christians after the great fire.

188. It is curious that Otto Procksch, working with entirely different assumptions about Paul's final Jerusalem journey in A.D. 55 and a subsequent Roman imprisonment, release, Spanish mission, and final Roman imprisonment, should also have concluded that A.D. 62 was the logical date for the execution: "Pauli Todesjahr 62 n. Chr.," *Luthertum*, 47 (1936), 225–235. His argument rests on the premises that Paul and Peter were not executed at the same time because their burial places were different; that the writing of 1 Peter implies a leadership vacuum in Rome during which Peter replaced Paul; and finally that the ascendency of Poppaea in 62 played a decisive role in the execution.

189. Cf. B. H. Warmington, *Nero: Reality and Legend* (New York: W. W. Norton, 1969), 50–51; J. G. F. Hind, "The Middle Years of Nero's Reign," *Historia* 20 (1971), 488–505; 501f. discusses the executions of Pallas and others in A.D. 62 but discounts the impact of the restored treason trials in an effort to show that the middle five years of Nero's reign,

60–65, were those referred to as exemplary by Trajan. Brassloff, "Claudia Octavia," *PW* 3, Part 2 (1899), 2893–2898, provides a detailed account of the complicated communications between the dates of the divorce and of Octavia's execution. Unfortunately he provides no precise chronology.

190. The significance of the early part of A.D. 62 for the disposition of Paul's case would be enhanced if Warmington is correct in sorting out the five conflicting versions of Nero's affair with Poppaea. He concludes that ". . . she did not attract Nero's interest till 62 and that the main tradition put the affair earlier in order to associate it with the murder of Agrippina." *Nero*, 47. If this is true, Poppaea would not have been in a position to tip the scales of justice in Paul's disfavor prior to 62.

CHAPTER III—INTERNALLY ASCERTAINABLE DATE-RANGES

1. Cf. W. J. Conybeare and J. W. Howson, *The Life and Epistles of St. Paul* (New York: Scribners, 1892), 219.

2. Ibid., 219.

3. C. Neumann and J. Partsch, *Physikalische Geographie von Griechenland mit besonderer Rücksicht auf das Alterthum* (Breslau: Wilhelm Koebner, 1885), 113–116; cf. Ellen Churchill Semple, *The Geography of the Mediterranean Region: Its Relation to Ancient History* (New York: AMS Press, 1971; repr. from the 1931 edition), 83–87; 579–582.

4. Suhl comes to a similar conclusion, *Chronologie*, 340.

5. J. Goudoever, *Biblical Calendars* (Leiden: Brill, 1959), 228ff.

6. Cf. Jeremias, *Eucharistic Words*, 36–41, for a fascinating account of the discussions between Schoch, Gerhardt, Fotheringham and the author on these technical questions.

7. Plooij, *Chronologie*, 85; cf. Goldstine, *New and Full Moons*, 88–89.

8. William Mitchell Ramsay, "A Fixed Date in the Life of St. Paul," *Exp* 5th Series, 3 (1896), 336–345.

9. Plooij, *Chronologie*, 83–85 .

10. Oswald Gerhardt, "In welchem Jahre wurde der Apostel Paulus in Jerusalem gefangen gesetzt?" *NKZ* 33 (1922), 89–114.

11. Theodor Zahn, *Die Apostelgeschichte des Lucas* (Leipzig: Deichert, 1919), 704f.

12. Haenchen, *Apostelgeschichte*, 516.

13. Ogg, *Chronology*, 140–145.

14. Julian Morgenstern, "The Reckoning of the Day in the Gospels and in Acts," *Crozer Quarterly* 26 (1949), 232–240.

15. Ogg, *Chronology*, 144–145; he fails to note the problems in this verse

related to the false motivation for the Jerusalem trip and the illogical excuse for bypassing Ephesus. Cf. Conzelmann, *Apostelgeschichte*, 116.

16. Cf. Chapter IV below.

17. W. P. Workman, "A New Date-Indication in Acts," *ET* 11 (1899–1900), 316–319.

18. Cf. Caesar, *Bell. Gall.* 4:36; 5:23.

19. Vegetius, *De re militari* 4:39; cf. Plooij, *Chronologie*, 86–88; Ogg, *Chronology*, 173–4; Parker and Dubberstein provide corrected figures for the Atonement Day fast in *Chronology*, 47.

20. Cf. the detailed discussion of Paul's journey to Rome in A. Breusing, *Die Nautik der Alten* (Bremen: Schünemann, 1886), 142–205; Hans Balmer, *Die Romfahrt des Apostels Paulus und die Seefahrtskunde im römischen Kaiserzeitalter* (Bern-Münchenbuchsee: Eugen Sutermeister, 1905) 269–510; a more recent discussion of maritime customs may be found in Jean Dauvillier, "A propos de la venue de saint Paul à Rome. Notes sur son procès et son voyage maritime," *BLE* 61 (1960), 3–26, esp. 18.

21. Cf. Plooij, *Chronologie*, 86; Billerbeck and Strack, *Kommentar*, 2, 771ff.

22. Conzelmann, *Apostelgeschichte*, 141, would seem to caution against making any such precise inferences because Acts 27:9–11 may be an editorial insertion. This assignment is made not on stylistic grounds but on the improbability of a conversation between Paul and the centurion on sailing strategy. No convincing reasons are adduced to show this to be impossible.

23. Cf. Ogg, *Chronology*, 173.

24. Cf. Breusing, *Nautik*; Balmer, *Romfahrt*; Ogg cites Pliny, "Spring opens the seas to navigation. It commences when the west winds soften the wintry air . . . on 8th February." *Chronology*, 175, but he comments that caution probably prevented departure till March.

25. Cf. Karl Georg Wieseler's account of the extensive debate on this issue up until the date of his commentary, *Commentar über den Brief Pauli an die Galater* (Göttingen: Dieterich, 1859), 90ff. A more recent investigation is by J. van Bruggen, *"Na veertien jaren:" De datering van het in Galaten 2 genoemde overleg te Jeruzalem* (Kampen: Kok, 1973), which continues the long effort by scholars to harmonize Acts and Galatians.

26. Cf. Wieseler, *Galater*, 91: "Aus chronologischer Verlegenheit haben nicht wenige Gelehrte (Cappellus, Grotius, Semmler, Heinrichs, Bertholdt, Künöl, Lüchler, Wurn, Ulrich, Böttger, früher auch Schott) für *de-*

*katessarōn tessarōn* schreiben wollen, allein gegen alle Handschriften. . . ."

27. Joseph Barber Lightfoot, *St. Paul's Epistle to the Galatians* (London: Macmillan, 1892), 102; Edgar Dewitt Burton, *A Critical and Exegetical Commentary on the Epistle to the Galatians* (Edinburgh: Clark, 1921), 68.

28. F. Sieffert, *Kritisch–exegetischer Kommentar über das Neue Testament. Der Brief an die Galater* (Göttingen: Vandenhoeck & Ruprecht, 1899), 77; Walter Bauer, *A Greek–English Lexicon of the New Testament and Other Early Christian Literature. A Translation and Adaptation by W. F. Arndt and W. F. Gingrich* (Chicago: University of Chicago Press, 1957), 178–179; C. Bruston argued that *dia* in Gal. 2:1 signifies "au cours de quatorze ans . . ." in "Les Dates principales de la vie de saint Paul de sa conversion à sa première épître," *Revue de théologie et des questions religieuses* 22 (1913) 125. Bruston concludes that while Paul wrote seventeen years after his conversion, his second visit to consult with Peter and James came sometime during the fourteen year span. S. Giet prefers the sense of "pendant" for *dia*, rendering Gal. 2:1 "Je montai à Jérusalem une nouvelle fois en quatorze ans." "Les trois premiers Voyages de saint Paul à Jérusalem," *RSR* 41 (1953), 334. Neither of these suggestions follows the precise sense of the Greek construction at this point; cf. Eduard Schwyzer, *Griechische Grammatik* (Munich: Beck, 1959, 3rd ed.), 550f.

29. Cf. the similar conclusion by Herman von Soden, "Chronology of the New Testament," *Encyclopaedia Biblica* 1, 813.

30. Bauer, *Lexicon*, 284.

31. J. H. Moulton and G. Milligan, *The Vocabulary of the Greek Testament* (London: Hodder & Stoughton, 1919), 231.

32. H. G. Liddell, R. Scott, and H. S. Jones, *A Greek–English Lexicon*, 9th ed. (Oxford, 1953), 615.

33. Cf. Eduard Schwartz, "Zur Chronologie des Paulus," *Gesammelte Schriften*, (Berlin: Gruyter, 1963) 5, 124–169, an essay which first appeared in 1907; William Mitchell Ramsay, "Numbers, Hours, and Years," *HDB* 5, 473–484.

34. Soden, *Encyclopaedia Biblica* 1, col 813; G. B. Caird, "Chronology of the NT," *IDB* 1, 606.

35. J. Frederick McCurdy, "Chronology," *JE* 4, 64–75.

36. Ramsay, *HDB* 5, 474.

37. C. Bruston, *Revue de théologie et des questions religieuses*, (1913), 135–139; Maurice Goguel, "La Vision de Paul à Corinth et sa Comparution devant Gallion: une Conjecture sur la Place Originale d'Actes, 18,

9–11," *RHPR* 12 (1932), 321–333; Stanislas Giet, "Nouvelles remarques sur les voyages de Saint Paul à Jérusalem," *RSR* 31 (1957), 340–342.

38. John Knox, "Fourteen Years Later: A Note on the Pauline Chronology," *JR* 16 (1936), 347; Buck and Taylor, *Saint Paul,* 222–226.

39. Knox, *Chapters,* 78, note 3.

40. Theodor Zahn, *Introduction to the New Testament,* tr. M. W. Jacobus (New York: Scribners, 1917, 2d ed.), ii; 461–463; Philipp Bachmann, *Der zweite Brief des Paulus an die Korinther* (Leipzig: Deichert, 1922), 391f.; E. B. Allo, *Saint Paul: Second Epître aux Corinthiens* (Paris: Lecoffre, 1956), 307; Gunther, *Chronology,* 26f. dates the transition "from Tarsus to Antioch" in the winter of A.D. 42–43, approximately fourteen years before the writing of 2 Cor. 10–13 in May of A.D. 56.

41. Merrill F. Unger, "Archeology and Paul's Tour of Cyprus," *BS* 117 (1960), 229.

42. Cf. Breusing, *Nautik,* 150–155; Balmer, *Romfahrt,* 286–295; Semple, *Geography,* 579–582.

43. Cf. Vegetius, *De re militari* 4:39; Pliny, *Natural History* 2:47; J. Rouge, "La Navigation hivernale sous l'Empire Romain," *Revue de Etudes Anciennes* 54 (1952), 316–325, discusses the literary and legal evidence, concluding that until the fourth century A.D., winter shipping was forbidden by custom and in the case of imperial transports, by law, from the end of October to the beginning of April. Thus the Vegetius calendar was apparently in effect: dangerous travel from March 10 through May 27 and from September 14 through November 11; sea closed from November 11 till March 10. Cf. William Mitchell Ramsay, "Roads and Travel in NT," *HDB* 5, 377.

44. Gustaf Dalman, *Arbeit und Sitte in Palästina* (Gütersloh: Bertelsmann, 1928), 1, 1, 156.

45. Cf. Breusing, *Nautik,* 159ff.; August Köster, *Das antike Seewesen* (Berlin: Schoetz & Parrhysius, 1923), 177–181, compares the speed and navigation of classical ships with those of more recent times.

46. *De re militari* 4:39; cf. Emile Delaye, "Routes et courriers aux temps de Saint Paul," *Etudes,* 131 (1912), 455.

47. Cf. Ramsay, *HDB* 5, 377.

48. Idem.

49. Cf. idem: "All travel across the mountains was avoided between the latter part of November and the latter part of March; and ordinary travellers, not forced by official duties, but free to choose their own time, would avoid the crossing between October (an extremely wet month on

the plateau) and May." Cf. also Franz X. Schaffer, *Cilicia,* (Gotha: Justus Perthes, 1903; *Ergänzungsheft No. 141 zu Petermanns Mitteilungen*), 104; Schaffer, "Die Kilikischen Hochpässe und Menons Zug über den Taurus," *Jahreshefte des Oesterreicheschen Archaeologischen Institut, Wien* (1901), 205f.

50. There are of course many studies like John W. Bailey's, "Paul's Second Missionary Journey," *Biblical World* 33 (1909), 414–423, which give only a cumulative total of time spent on the trip without reckoning things out in detail, a procedure which makes them useless for chronological consideration.

51. Cf. Julius Wellhausen, "Kritische Analyse der Apostelgeschichte," *Abhandlungen der Königlichen Gesellschaft der Wissenschaft zu Göttingen* 15 (1914), 30f.: "Paulus ist nach der Rückkehr von Jerusalem noch eine ganze Weile in Antiochia geblieben. . . . Die Reise in 16,1–10 muss ein paar Jahre gedauert haben und beschwerlich genug gewesen sein."

52. See the standard Galatians commentaries for a discussion of the North/South Galatian debate; I concur with North Galatian advocates and assume the congregations were located in Ancyra, Pessimus, and perhaps Germa, since Paul addresses them in Gal. 3:1 with the title "Galatians." Cf. Franz Mussner's discussion in *Der Galaterbrief* (Freiburg: Herder, 1974), 1–8. The suggestion by Lake and Haenchen, that Paul visited only the cities of Cotiaeum and Dorylaeum, is unacceptable because these cities were not in Galatia at all. Cf. W. M. Calder and G. E. Bean, *A Classical Map of Asia Minor* (Ankara: The British Institute of Archeology, 1958), and David Magie, *Roman Rule in Asia Minor* (Princeton: Princeton University Press, 1950), 1, 453ff.

53. This estimate is worked out on the basis of Westermann's *Atlas zur Weltgeschichte* (Braunschweig: 1956), 38–39; William Mitchell Ramsay, *The Historical Geography of Asia Minor* (Amsterdam: Hakkert, 1962, 2d ed.); Ramsay, *St. Paul the Traveller and Roman Citizen* (London: Hodder & Stoughton, 1920); Lake, *Beginnings,* 5, 224ff.; Calder and Bean, *Classical Map.* Distances are reckoned in part from F. von Caucig, *Kurt Schroeders Reiseführer Turkei* (Bonn: 1961). Cf. Konrad Miller, *Itineraria Romana: Römische Reisewege an der Hand der Tabula Peutingeriana* (Rome: L'Erma di Bretschneider, 1964; repr. of the 1916 ed.) for a comparison for individual sections of the itinerary.

54. Martin P. Charlesworth, *Trade–Routes and Commerce in the Roman Empire* (Cambridge: University Press, 1924), 86, provides some basis for estimating the speed of travel in Asia Minor. He notes that the

journey from Ephesus to the Euphrates on the main trade route through Laodicea, Philomelium, Iconium, Mazaca, and Melitene would take a person on foot about 35 days and a horseman about 30 days. Since this distance is an estimated 1083 kilometers, the average speed for a normal walker per day would be 30.9 kilometers. Charlesworth notes that shorter distances were normally covered at a greater rate of speed, e.g., from Ephesus to Tralles in one day (45 kilometers) or from Mazaca to the Cilician Gates in six days (240 kilometers). Cf. also Ramsay, *HDB* 5, 375–402; Delaye, *Etudes* 131 (1912) 455–457. Lionel Casson suggests that the normal traveler without government facilities ". . . did about fifteen to twenty miles a day on foot, some twenty–five to thirty in a carriage. Forty, even forty–five was possible but it meant an exhaustingly long and hard day's travel." *Travel in the Ancient World* (Toronto: Hakkert, 1974), 189.

55. Gal. 2:11ff. indicates that Peter arrived after Paul, that he ate with the gentiles for some time, that word got back to Jerusalem regarding his apostasy, and that a representative of James was sent to censure him. It would seem to require at least two months for the completion of these journeys over the 600 kilometer distance between Antioch and Jerusalem; four months would be a more normal estimate. For a detailed defense of the sequence reported in Galatians in which the conflict with Peter followed immediately after the Apostolic Conference, cf. Ogg, *Chronology*, 89–98. H. M. Féret, *Pierre et Paul à Antioche et à Jérusalem. Le 'Conflit' des deux Apôtres* (Paris: Editions du Cerf, 1955), takes the implausible step of reversing the sequence in Galatians to place the conflict before the Apostolic Conference. For a detailed criticism of Feret's conclusions, see Jacques Dupont, "Pierre et Paul à Antioche et à Jérusalem," *RSR* 45 (1957), 42–60; 255–259.

56. Eduard Meyer, *Ursprung und Anfänge des Christentums* 3, 84, 169, concurs in seeing that the second missionary journey demands three years. He allows the period from A.D. 47–50 for these travels and activities.

57. The minimum estimate is on the basis of 40 kilometers per day, with no provision for travel delays.

58. The normal estimate is on the basis of 30 kilometers per day, with occasional stopovers on longer journeys and delays at points demanded by evidence in Acts and the letters.

59. Distance estimated from modern highway in *Schroeder's Reiseführer.*

60. Estimated from Calder and Bean, *Classical Map.*

61. Estimated from Calder and Bean, *Classical Map.*

62. Distance on modern highway from Konya to the approximate site of Pisidian Antioch is 146 k.; the estimate on the basis of Calder and Bean, *Classical Map* is 142 k. The shorter distance is selected here to give the 18 months theory the benefit of the doubt, and it is possible that all the Calder and Bean estimates are similarly shorter than actual road conditions.

63. Estimated from Calder and Bean, *Classical Map*.

64. Distance reckoned from modern road from Ankara to Kuetahya in *Schroeder's Reiseführer*.

65. Distance reckoned from ibid. on modern roads between Kuetahya and Simav, the approximate site of Ancyra Sidera; the distance is estimated to Sindirgi and from there by modern road to the site of Troas. The road system corresponding to the details in Acts 16:7-8 has not been systematically examined, judging from the gaps in the Calder and Bean *Classical Map* and the vague dotted lines that continue to appear in biblical atlas maps of Paul's journeys. The methods developed by S. Frederick Starr, "Mapping Ancient Roads in Anatolia," *Archeology* 16 (1963), 162-169 and D. H. French, "A Study of Roman Roads in Anatolia," *Anatolian Studies* 24 (1974), 143-149 should be applied to this terrain.

66. Cf. Ramsay, *Traveller*, 234.

CHAPTER IV—TESTING CHRONOLOGIES

1. J. B. Lightfoot, "A Chronology of St. Paul's Life and Epistles," *Biblical Essays* (London: Macmillan, 1893), 215-233, citation from 215.

2. Harnack, *Chronologie*, 233ff.; *Biblical World* (1897), 285-391.

3. Harnack, *Chronologie*, 237.

4. Harnack, *Sitzungsberichte* (1912), 680-682.

5. Gustav Hoennicke, *Die Chronologie des Lebens des Apostels Paulus* (Leipzig: Deichert, 1903).

6. W. J. Conybeare and J. S. Howson, *The Life and Epistles of St. Paul* (London: 1892), 821ff.

7. C. H. Turner, "Chronology of the New Testament," *HDB* 1, 403-426.

8. H. Leclercq, "Paul (Saint)," *DACL* 13, 2568-2699.

9. Erich Fascher, "Paulus (Apostel)," *PWSup* 8 (1956), cols 431-466.

10. Ernst Haenchen, *Die Apostelgeschichte* (Göttingen: Vandenhoeck & Ruprecht, 1961, 13th ed.), 480, note 6; his discussion of the problem of chronology is on 53ff.

11. Dieter Georgi, *Die Geschichte der Kollekte des Paulus für Jerusalem* (Hamburg–Bergstedt: Reich, 1965), 91-96.

12. J. Cambier, "Paul (Vie et Doctrine de Saint)," *DBSup* 7 (1962), 279–387; idem "The Life and Work of St. Paul," *Introduction to the New Testament*, ed. A. Robert & A. Feuillet; translated by Skehen, et al (New York: Deschée, 1965), 373–380; idem "Le Voyage de S. Paul à Jérusalem en Act. ix. 26ss. et le Schéma Missionaire Théologique de S. Luc," *NTS* 8 (1961–62), 249–257.

13. Cambier, *Introduction*, 373–380.

14. George Ogg, *The Chronology of the Life of Paul* (London: Epworth, 1968).

15. Ibid., 113, 115.

16. Ibid., 56f.

17. Günther Bornkamm, *Paul*, tr. M. G. Stalker (New York: Harper, 1971); C. J. Cadoux, "A Tentative Synthetic Chronology of the Apostolic Age," *JBL* 56 (1937), 177–191; Philip Carrington, *The Early Christian Church*, 1: *The First Christian Century* (Cambridge: University Press, 1957); F. A. Christie, "Harnack's Chronology of the New Testament," *The New World*, 6 (1897), 451–467; Carl Clemen, *Die Chronologie des Paulinischen Briefe* (Halle: Max Niemeyer, 1893); Hans Conzelmann, *Geschichte des Urchristentums* (Göttingen: Vandenhoeck & Ruprecht, 1971, 2nd ed.); Charles H. Dodd, "Chronology of the Acts and the Pauline Epistles," in A. W. F. Blunt, et al, *Oxford Helps to the Study of the Bible* (New York: Oxford University Press, 1931, 2nd ed.), 195–197; Frederick William Farrar, *The Life and Work of St. Paul* (New York: Dutton, 1902); Floyd Vivian Filson, *A New Testament History* (Philadelphia: Westminster Press, 1964); Jack Finegan, *Handbook of Biblical Chronology* (Princeton: University Press, 1964); Stanislas Giet, "Les trois premiers Voyages de saint Paul à Jérusalem," *RSR* 41 (1953), 321–347; idem, "Traditions chronologiques légendaires ou historiques," *Studia Patristica* 1: *Papers Presented to the Second International Conference on Patristic Studies held at Christ Church, Oxford, 1955.* Part I. ed. K. Aland and F. L. Cross (Berlin: Akademie-Verlag, 1957), 607–620; Leonhard Goppelt, *The Apostolic and Post–Apostolic Times*, tr. R. A. Guelich (New York: Harper, 1970); Donald Guthrie, *New Testament Introduction: The Pauline Epistles* (London: Tyndale, 1961); Gilmore H. Guyot, "The Chronology of St. Paul," *CBQ* 6 (1944), 28–36; Joachim Jeremias, "Sabbathjahr und neutestamentliche Chronologie," *ZNW* 27 (1928), 98–103; Maurice Jones, "A New Chronology of the Life of St. Paul," *Exp*, Series 8, 17 (1919), 363–383; 424–446; 18 (1919), 99–120; Adolf Jülicher, *An Introduction to the New Testament*, tr. J. P. Ward (London: Smith, Elder, 1904); Werner G.

Kümmel, *Feine–Behm Einleitung in das neue Testament* (Heidelberg: Quelle & Meyer, 1963, 12th ed.); Joseph Barber Lightfoot, "A Chronology of St. Paul's Life and Epistles," *Biblical Essays* (London: Macmillan, 1893), 213–233; Willi Marxsen, *Einleitung in das neue Testament: Eine Einführung in ihre Probleme* (Gütersloh: Gerd Mohn, 1963); A. H. McNeile, *St. Paul: His Life, Letters, and Christian Doctrine* (Cambridge: University Press, 1920); Bruce Manning Metzger, *The New Testament, Its Background, Growth, and Content* (Nashville: Abingdon, 1965); Wilhelm Michaelis, *Einleitung in das neue Testament: Die Entstehung, Sammlung und Überlieferung der Schriften des neuen Testaments* (Bern: Berchtold Haller, 1961, 3rd ed.); James Moffatt, *An Introduction to the Literature of the New Testament* (Edinburgh: T. & T. Clark, 1918, 3rd ed.); Dale Moody, "A New Chronology for the Life and Letters of Paul," *Perspectives in Religious Studies* 3 (1976), 248–271; Johannes Müller-Bardorff, *Paulus: Wege zu didaktischer Erschliessung der paulinischen Briefe* (Gütersloh: Gerd Mohn, 1970); Arthur Darby Nock, *St. Paul* (New York: Harper, 1938); F. Prat, "La Chronologie de l'âge apostolique," *RSR* 3 (1912), 374–392; Otto Procksch, "Pauli Todesjahr 62 n. Chr.," *Luthertum* 47 (1936), 225–235; Bo Reicke, *The New Testament Era*, tr. D. E. Green (Philadelphia: Fortress, 1968); Beda Rigaux, *The Letters of St. Paul: Modern Studies*, tr. S. Yonick (Chicago: Franciscan Herald Press, 1968); B. W. Robinson, *The Life of Paul* (London: Cambridge University Press, 1927); John A. T. Robinson, *Redating the New Testament* (London: SCM, 1976); H. Rongy, "Chronologie des voyages de S. Paul," *Revue ecclésiastique de Liège* 22 (1930–31), 30–35; idem, "Les épîtres de S. Paul dans l'ordre chronologique," *Revue ecclésiastique de Liège* 22 (1930–31), 89–94; Donald Joseph Selby, *Toward the Understanding of St. Paul* (Englewood Cliffs: Prentice–Hall, 1962); Clyde W. Votaw, "Inductive Studies in the Acts: Outline of the Primitive Era of Christianity: As Recorded in the Acts of the Apostles: 30–63 A.D.," *Biblical World* 9 (1897), 45–47; idem, "Recent Discussions of the Chronology of the Apostolic Age," *Biblical World*, 11 (1898), 112–119; 177–187; Dawson Walker, "St. Paul's Visits to Jerusalem, as Recorded in the Acts and in the Epistle to the Galatians," *The Gift of Tongues and Other Essays* (Edinburgh: T. & T. Clark, 1906), 177–214; Johannes Weiss, *Earliest Christianity: A History of the Period* A.D. *30–150*, tr. F. C. Grant (New York: Harpers, 1959); Karl Heinrich Weizsäcker, *The Apostolic Age of the Christian Church*, tr. J. Millar (New York: Putnams, 1894); Johannes Welser, "Zur Chronologie des Paulus," *TQ* 80 (1898), 353–379; Friedrich Westberg, *Zur*

*Neutestamentlichen Chronologie und Golgothas Ortslage* (Leipzig: Deichert, 1911); Theodor Zahn, *Introduction to the New Testament*, tr. directed by M. W. Jacobus (New York: Scribners, 1917, 2nd ed.).

18. Eduard Schwartz, "Zur Chronologie des Paulus," *Gesammelte Schriften* (Berlin: Gruyter, 1963) 5, 124–169; the essay first appeared in 1907 in *Nachrichten von der königlichen Gesellschaft der Wissenschaft zu Göttingen: Philologisch–historische Klasse* (1907), 269–274.

19. Ibid., 162.

20. Eduard Meyer, *Ursprung und Anfänge des Christentums* (Berlin: Cotta, 1923, 2nd ed.), 3, 35ff., 169ff.

21. William Mitchell Ramsay, "Pauline Chronology," *Exp*, 5th Series, 5 (1897), 201–211; "A Second Fixed Point in Pauline Chronology," *Exp* 6 (1900), 88–105; *Pauline and Other Studies in Early Christian History* (London: Hodder & Stoughton, 1906); *St. Paul the Traveller and Roman Citizen* (London: 1920).

22. Daniel Plooij, *De Chronologie van het Leven van Paulus* (Leiden: Brill, 1918). A detailed critique is provided by F. W. Grosheide, "De Chronologie van het leven van Paulus," *Gereformeed Theologisch Tijdschrift* 19 (1918–19), 349–361.

23. Lake, "The Chronology of Acts," *Beginnings*, 5, 445–474.

24. John J. Gunther, *Paul: Messenger and Exile: A Study in the Chronology of His Life and Letters* (Valley Forge: Judson, 1972), 25.

25. Ibid., 26.

26. Ibid., note 3, 169.

27. S. Dockx, "Chronologie de la Vie de Saint Paul depuis sa Conversion Jusqu'à son Séjour à Rome," *NovT* 13 (1971), 261–304; idem, *Chronologies néotestamentaires et vie de l'Eglise primitive: Recherches exégétiques* (Gembloux: Duculot, 1977).

28. Cf. Dockx's detailed reconstruction of the period just prior to Paul's departure for Jerusalem in "Chronologie Paulinienne de l'Année de la Grand Collecte," *RB* 81 (1973), 183–195.

29. Alfred Suhl, *Paulus und seine Briefe: Ein Beitrag zur paulinischen Chronologie* (Gütersloh: Mohn, 1975), 91.

30. Ibid., 321.

31. Ibid., 315.

32. Ibid., 27ff.

33. Ibid., 341f.

34. Wacholder, *IDBSup*, 762f.; a more extensive statement of his findings is provided in *HUCA*, (1973), 153–196 and (1975), 201–218.

35. Plooij, *Chronologie*, 83ff.; Goldstine, *New and Full Moons*, 89.

36. Joseph Aberle, "Chronologie des Apostels Paulus von seiner Bekehrung bis zur Abfassung des Galaterbriefes (37–57 n. Chr.)," *BZ* 1 (1903), 256–279; 372–377; Benjamin Wisner Bacon, "The Chronological Scheme of Acts," *HTR* 14 (1921) 137–166; idem, "A Criticism of the New Chronology of Paul," *Exp*, 5th Series, 7 (1898), 123–136; 10 (1899), 351–367; 412–430; Herbert Braun, "Christentum, Entstehung," *RGG* 3rd ed. 1, cols 1685–1695; Ch. Bruston, "Les Dates principales de la vie de saint Paul de sa conversion à sa première épître," *Revue de théologie et des questions religieuses* 22 (1913), 122–140; Morton Scott Enslin, *Christian Beginnings* (New York: Harper, 1938); Maurice Goguel, "Essai sur la chronologie paulinienne," *RHR* 65 (1912), 285–339; Harold Hoehner, *Chronology of the Apostolic Age* (Dallas Theological Seminary Dissertation, 1965); Charles King, "The Outlines of New Testament Chronology," *CQR* 139 (1945), 129–153; Alfred Loisy, *L'Epître aux Galates* (Paris: Emile Nourry, 1916); Arthur Cushman McGiffert, *A History of Christianity in the Apostolic Age* (New York: Scribner, 1922); Hermann von Soden, "Chronology of the New Testament," *Encyclopaedia Biblica* 1, cols 799–819; Karl Thieme, "Le Plan des 'Actes des Apôtres' et la chronologie de son contenu," *Dieu Vivant* 26 (1954), 127–133; E. A. Thorne, "The Earlier Missionary Journeys in Acts of Apostles," *CQR* 121 (1935–36), 109–117; Stanley D. Toussaint, "The Chronological Problem of Galatians 2, 1–10," *BS* 120 (1963), 334–340; Philipp Vielhauer, *Geschichte der urchristlichen Literatur* (Berlin: de Gruyter, 1965); Valentin Weber, *Die Abfassung des Galaterbriefes vor dem Apostelkonzil* (Ravensburg: 1900); idem, "Die sechs Jerusalembesuche des Apostels Paulus," *Theologisch–praktische Monats–Schrift* 26 (1916), 285–289; actually Weber maintains that the Galatians 2 visit occurred between Paul's visits reported in Acts 11 and Acts 15; Julius Wellhausen, "Zur Chronologie des Paulus," *Nachrichten von der königlichen Gesellschaft der Wissenschaften zu Göttingen; Philologisch–historische Klasse* (Berlin: Weidmannsche Buchhandlung, 1907), 269–274; idem, "Noten zur Apostelgeschichte," *Nachrichten* (1907), 1–21.

37. Donald W. Riddle, *Paul: Man of Conflict: A Modern Biographical Sketch* (Nashville: Cokesbury, 1940); and Harold H. Hutson, *New Testament Life and Literature* (Chicago: University of Chicago, 1946), 117–148.

38. Riddle, *Conflict*, 76.

39. Cf. Dieter Georgi, "Corinthians, Second," *IDBSup*, 183–186.

40. John C. Hurd, Jr., *The Origin of I Corinthians* (New York: Seabury,

1965); idem, "Pauline Chronology and Pauline Theology," *Christian History and Interpretation: Studies Presented to John Knox,* ed. W. R. Farmer, et al (New York: Cambridge University Press, 1967), 225–248.

41. John C. Hurd, Jr., "The Sequence of Paul's Letters," *CJT* 14 (1968), 189–200.

42. Ibid., 198.

43. Hurd, *Corinthians,* 240–274.

44. Charles Henry Buck and Greer Taylor, *Saint Paul. A Study of the Development of His Thought* (New York: Scribners, 1969).

45. Udo Borse, *Der Standort des Galaterbriefes* (Cologne: Hanstein, 1972); for still another picture of the "development" cf. Wolfgang Wiefel, "Die Hauptrichtung des Wandels in eschatologischen Denken des Paulus," *BZ* 30 (1974), 65–81.

46. Cf. Victor Paul Furnish, "Development in Paul's Thought," *JAAR* 38 (1970), 289–303.

47. Cf. Robert Jewett, *Paul's Anthropological Terms. A Study of Their Use in Conflict Settings* (Leiden: Brill, 1971), 10.

48. Buck and Taylor, *Saint Paul,* 46–52; cf. the discussion of their argument in Chapter II.

49. Ibid., 214.

50. Ibid., 214.

51. John Knox, "Fourteen Years Later, a Note on the Pauline Chronology," *JR* 16 (1936), 341–349; idem, "The Pauline Chronology," *JBL* 58 (1939), 15–40; idem, *Chapters in a Life of Paul* (New York: Abingdon, 1950).

52. Knox, *Chapters,* 68f.

53. Knox argued that "the context strongly indicates that the 'church' (referred to in Acts 18:22) was there (in Jerusalem)." Ibid., 68. Haenchen admits the force of this argument in *Apostelgeschichte,* 480, but seeks to avoid the conclusion that Paul had planned to visit Jerusalem at this time. He notes that Paul started out for "Syria" (Acts 18:18) and ended up in Caesarea (18:22). This is explained by the presence of a northeast wind: "Im Sommer herrscht ein starker Nordostwind vor . . . , der eine Fahrt nach Selucia, dem Hafen Antiochas, vorbot und den Umweg über Caesarea erzwang"; 483. He derived this idea from Lake and Cadbury, *Beginnings,* 4, 231 although no real proof is offered there either. In reality the prevailing wind in the eastern Mediterranean in high summer is from the west. Hans Balmer showed there is a steady west wind during July and August on this part of the sea, drawing his information from

ancient and modern ship journals; *Romfahrt*, 293f. Confirmation is drawn by Balmer from Acts 27:4 which describes the problem caused by this west wind in the same part of the sea; cf. 288f. It may be that Foakes-Jackson, Cadbury, and Haenchen confused the summer etesian which blows out of the north or northeast in Aegean waters with the wind conditions in the eastern Mediterranean.

54. Knox, *Chapters*, 53ff.; Nickle, *Collection*, 111ff. stresses this aspect of the rationale for the Jerusalem offering.

55. Knox, *Chapters*, 76.

56. Cf. Haenchen, *Apostelgeschichte*, 60, note 480; George Ogg, "A New Chronology of Saint Paul's Life," *ET* 67 (1955–56), 120–123; Thomas H. Campbell, "Paul's Missionary Journeys as Reflected in His Letters," *JBL* 74 (1955), 80–87; Guthrie, *Pauline Epistles*, 279–281. On the other hand, Knox was supported by Donald Rowlingson, "The Jerusalem Conference and Jesus' Nazareth Visit," *JBL* 71 (1952), 69–74, although he alters Knox's dating system, setting the Apostolic Conference in 52 and the conversion in 37. This is something of an improvement over Knox's system, but it still places the conversion too late to accommodate the Aretas datum. Paul S. Minear provided independent confirmation of the Knox method by correlating details concerning the Jerusalem collection activities in "The Jerusalem Fund and Pauline Chronology," *ATR*, 25 (1943), 389–396.

57. Knox, *Chapters*, 78.

58. Karl Georg Wieseler, *Commentar über den Brief Pauli an die Galater* (Göttingen: Dieterischen Buchhandlung, 1859), 553ff.; *Chronologie des apostolischen Zeitalters* (Göttingen: Vandenhoeck & Ruprecht, 1848), 201ff. As predecessors in the identification of Gal. 2:1 with Acts 18:22 he names Chrysostomus, Luther, Capelle, Whiston, van Til, Hess, Koehler, and as followers of his own chronology he names Huther and Lutterbeck.

59. Note Haenchen's unfortunate attempt to place Wieseler and Knox in the same pro–Lukan camp in *Apostelgeschichte*, 480.

60. Gustav Volkmar, *Paulus von Damaskus bis zum Galaterbrief* (Zurich: Schroeter & Meyer, 1887), 26ff. provides the reprint of his article of 1884.

61. Ernst Barnikol, *Die drei Jerusalem Reisen des Paulus. Die echte Konkordanz der Paulusbriefe mit der Wir-Quelle der Apostelgeschichte* (Kiel: Mühlau, 1929); idem, "Die Mission des Paulus," *Apostolische und Neutestamentliche Dogmengeschichte als Vor–Dogmengeschichte* (Halle:

Akademischer Verlag, 1938), 74–75; idem, "Kam Paulus vor Pfingsten zu Petrus? Die Entstehung der Hellenisten-Gemeinde in Jerusalem nach 40 n. Chr. um 42 n. Chr. und ihre Zerstreuung nach dem Martyrium des Stephanus vor 45 n. Chr. um 44 n. Chr.," *Theologische Jahrbücher* (1956), 16–20.

62. Gerd Lüdemann, *Paulus der Heidenapostel: I. Studien zur Chronologie* (Göttingen Habilitationsschrift, 1977); publication in the FRLANT series is anticipated for 1979.

63. Ibid., 107.

64. Cf. Gerhard Friedrich, *Der Brief an die Philipper: Das Neue Testament Deutsch*, 8 (Göttingen: Vandenhoeck & Ruprecht, 1976, 14th ed.), 173.

65. Lüdemann, *Chronologie*, 216.

66. Cf. Jewett, *Paul's Anthropological Terms*.

67. Wolfgang Wiefel, "Die jüdische Gemeinschaft im antiken Rom und die Anfänge des römischen Christentume: Bemerkungen zu Anlass und Zweck des Römerbriefs," *Jud* 26 (1970), 65–88.

68. Lüdemann, *Chronologie*, 274.

69. Ibid., 142–151.

70. S. Applebaum, "The Organization of the Jewish Communities in the Diaspora," *The Jewish People in the First Century*, ed. S. Safrai & M. Stern (Philadelphia: Fortress, 1974), 1, 464–503, esp. 492ff.

71. Cf. Hans Dieter Betz, "The Literary Composition and Function of Paul's Letter to the Galatians," NTS 21 (1974–75), 353–379.

72. Cf. Hans Conzelmann and Andreas Lindemann, *Arbeitsbuch zum Neuen Testament* (Tübingen: Mohr-Siebeck, 1976, 2nd ed.), 413.

73. Lüdemann, *Chronologie*, 73.

74. Cf. Traugott Holtz's analysis of the significance of the Apostolic Conference in relation to the conflict with Peter at Antioch, *NovT* (1974), 115–123.

75. Cf. Bauer, *Lexicon*, 592.

76. Lüdemann, *Chronologie*, 160.

77. J. van Bruggen, *"Na veertien jaren:" De datering von het in Galaten 2 genoemde overleg te Jeruzalem* (Kampen: Kok, 1973); Frederic R. Crownfield, *A Historical Approach to the New Testament* (New York: Harper, 1960); Lyn Howard Ramsey, *The Place of Galatians in the Career of Paul* (Columbia University Dissertation, 1960); W. Smith, "The Chronology of Acts and Epistles," *The London Quarterly and Holborn Review*, Series 6, 23 (1954), 270–276.

78. The impossible dilemmas posed by the compromise chronologies were documented more than twenty years ago when G. B. Caird pointed out the flaws of each option and then left the entire problem up in the air; *The Apostolic Age* (London: Duckworth, 1955), 198–210; this appendix was reprinted under the title "Chronology of the NT," in *IDB* 1, 599–607.

CHAPTER V—CAUSES OF THE CHRONOLOGICAL DILEMMA

1. John C. Hurd, Jr. provides an extensive discussion of the harmonizing hypotheses in *The Origin of I Corinthians* (New York: Seabury, 1965), 35ff. Caird analyzes the major compromise solutions in *IDB* 1, 599–607, noting the major faults in each alternative.

2. C. J. Cadoux, "A Tentative Synthetic Chronology of the Apostolic Age," *JBL* 56 (1937), 177–191.

3. F. F. Bruce, "Galatian Problems. 1. Autobiographical Data," *BJRL* 51 (1968–69), 292–309.

4. Cf. Robert G. Hoerber, "Galatians 2:10 and the Acts of the Apostles," *CTM* 31 (1960), 482–491; Charles H. Talbert, "Again: Paul's Visits to Jerusalem," *NovT* 9 (1967), 26–40; R. Liechtenhan, "Die Beiden ersten Besuche des Paulus in Jerusalem," *Harnack–Ehrung: Beiträge zur Kirchengeschichte, ihrem lehrer Adolf von Harnack zu seinem siebzigsten geburtstag (7. Mai 1921) dargebracht* (Leipzig: Hinrichs, 1921), 51–67.

5. Maurice Goguel, *The Birth of Christianity*, tr. H. C. Snape (London: Allen & Unwin, 1953), 292ff.

6. Ibid., 186ff.; D. R. De Lacey, "Paul in Jerusalem," *NTS* 20 (1973–74), 82–86, goes even farther in Goguel's direction, identifying the Galatians 2 visit with Acts 9 and placing the Apostolic Conference in A.D. 45. In addition to the insurmountable difficulties he shares with Goguel, there are the resultant silence in Acts about the acquaintance visit of Gal. 1:18, the contradictions in personnel and rationale between Acts 9 and Galatians 2, and the necessity to date Galatians before any of the Galatian churches, north or south, had received the gospel.

7. Meyer, *Ursprung* 3, 169ff.

8. Schwartz, *Gesammelte Schriften*, 124ff.

9. Lake, *Beginnings*, 5, 445–474.

10. Stanley D. Toussaint reaches a similar conclusion in his effort to find a solution which does not need ". . . to accuse either Luke or Paul of errors or inaccuracies." "The Chronological Problem of Galatians 2:1–10," *BS* 120 (1963), 334–340; citation from 335.

11. Jeremias, *ZNW* 27 (1928), 98–103.

12. S. Dockx, "Chronologie de la Vie de Saint Paul depuis sa Conversion Jusqu'à son Séjour à Rome," *NovT* 13 (1971), 261–304; Pierre Benoît, "La deuxième visite de saint Paul à Jérusalem," *Biblica* 40 (1959), 778–792.

13. Zahn, *Introduction*, 481ff.; Plooij, *Chronologie*, 129ff.; Guthrie, *Pauline Epistles*, 278.

14. Pierson Parker, "Once More Acts and Galatians," *JBL* 86 (1967), 175–182.

15. Cf. Benjamin Wisner Bacon, "Acts versus Galatians: the Crux of Apostolic History," *AJT* 11 (1907), 456.

16. Cf. Haenchen, *Apostelgeschichte*, 319–323; Conzelmann, *Apostelgeschichte*, 68f.; and Georg Strecker, "Die sogenannte zweite Jerusalemreise des Paulus (Acts 11, 27–30)," *ZNW* 53 (1962), 67–77, who come to the same negative conclusion on redaction critical grounds. Strecker summarizes: "Die Fiction der Paulusreise ist durchaus der absicht eingeordnet, die heilsgeschichtliche Kontinuität zu demonstrieren"; 77. The basis for this conclusion was set forth clearly by Dibelius' *Theologische Literaturzeitung* article of 1947, repr. as pp. 93–101 of *Studies*.

17. Kümmel, *Einleitung*, 179; Goppelt, *Times*, 222; Haenchen, *Apostelgeschichte*, 58; Conzelmann, *Apostelgeschichte*, 87; Georgi, *Kollekte*, 94; Ogg, *Chronology*, 200; Gunther, *Chronology*, 13f.; Dockx, *NovT* (1971), 303; Fascher, *PWSup* 8, cols 431–466.

18. Marxsen, *Einleitung*, 25; Michaelis, *Einleitung*, 153; Guthrie, *Epistles*, 278; Filson, *History*, 398; Giet, *RSR* (1953), 345; Müller-Bardorff, *Paulus*, 112; Cambier, *DBSup* 7, 279–387.

19. Harnack, *Chronologie*, 1, 237.

20. Meyer, *Ursprung*, 3, 84; Lake, *Beginnings*, 5, 470.

21. Cf. Chapter III.

22. F. F. Bruce, "Paul and Jerusalem," *Tyndale Bulletin* 19 (1968), 25.

23. Solomon Zeitlin, "Paul's Journeys to Jerusalem," *JQR* 57 (1967), 173.

CHAPTER VI—EXPERIMENTAL HYPOTHESIS

1. Hurd, "Pauline Chronology," *IDB Sup*, 167. The final item of "Imprisonment and Execution" on Hurd's outline is not directly attested by the authentic Pauline letters, and consequently cannot be allowed to play a decisive role in the creation of the basic framework of time–spans in the current experiment.

2. Cf. Lake, *Beginnings*, 5, 464; Plooij, *Chronologie*, 44, 173f.; Meyer,

*Ursprung*, 37; Otto Bauernfeind, *Die Apostelgeschichte* (Leipzig: Deichert, 1939), 226: "Bald nach dem Gallio–Verfahren verlässt Paulus Korinth, *post hoc*, nicht *propter hoc*."

3. Cf. Chapter II.

4. Cf. note 2 above.

5. 1 Thess. 3:1ff. is illustrative of Paul's custom.

6. Cf. Knox, *Chapters*, 80.

7. The word *anabeinō* is a technical term in the NT for the trip to Jerusalem; cf. Matt. 20:17–18; Mark 10:32; Luke 2:4, 42; 18:10; 19:28; John 2:13; 5:1; 11:55; 7:8; 10:14; Acts 3:1; 11:2; 21:12, 15; 24:11; 25:1, 9. Johannes Schneider, *"Bainō, anabainō, ktl,"* *TWNT* 1, cols 516–521, shows that this word and its Hebrew counterpart have a cultic significance throughout biblical and rabbinic usage. He cites Schlatter's statement that *ala/anabeinein* is the technical category for the approach to Jerusalem or to the temple.

8. Ramsay, *Traveller*, 294, reckons a two week period for the comparable journey from Troas to Tyre (Acts 20:13–21:3).

9. The rendezvous of three traveling missionaries such as Paul, Titus, and Barnabas could scarcely have been accidental. The question of whether the gentile Christians must be circumcised was so crucial for Paul and the Antioch church that we must assume there were advance arrangements for the Jerusalem parley.

10. Using the classical definition of probability as outlined in a standard manual such as Murray R. Spiegel, *Theory and Problems of Statistics* (New York: Schaum, 1961), 99f., the following formula is applicable: "the probability of occurrence of $E_1$, $E_2$, and $E_3$ is equal to the probability of $E_1$ times the probability of $E_2$ given that $E_1$ has occurred, times the probability of $E_3$ given that both $E_1$ and $E_2$ have occurred." The odds that the Gallio date fell on the right year in the relevant period from A.D. 30–52 are 1:23; the same odds pertain to the Claudius edict falling on the right year within the 23 year period; the two year Aretas span produces odds of 2:23; the alternative dates provided by Harnack's calculation of the date of the conversion, reckoned on the basis of the month rather than the day, produces the odds of 1:156. In this instance $E_1$ times $E_2$ times $E_3$ times $E_4$ produces the probability of 1:474–591.

11. Cf. Conzelmann, *Apostelgeschichte*, 133; Munck, *Acts*, 232–235; Haenchen, *Apostelgeschichte*, 60–64, 591, suggests that Luke may have misunderstood his source, which perhaps related the two year period to Felix's tenure. The reason for this supposition is obvious: Haenchen's

chronology has Paul make the final Jerusalem journey in A.D. 55 and depart in the fall of the same year for Rome. There is no room in this scheme for a two year Caesarean imprisonment. For a discussion of the historical problem, cf. Chapter II.

12. Cf. Chapter III.

13. Cf. Chapter II.

14. For the May 29, 57, date of Pentecost, cf. the calendar in Chapter III, 2nd section. Ramsay, *Traveller*, 294, lays out a typical case for Paul's arrival by Pentecost.

15. Cf. Haenchen, *Apostelgeschichte*, 102f.; Bornkamm, *Studies in Luke-Acts*, 198.

16. Cf. Haenchen, *Apostelgeschichte*, 521; Georgi, *Kollekte*, 89.

17. Acts 20:3; cf. Georgi, *Kollekte*, 85–88.

18. Cf. Chapter II.

19. Cf. Chapter II.

20. Cf. Chapter II.

21. Cf. Chapter III.

22. Cf. the reconstruction of events in Chapter III.

23. Cf. Plooij, *Chronologie*, 168f.

24. Cf. Chapter II.

25. The probabilities are reckoned on three assumptions, that the relevant base period is twelve years, from A.D. 53–64, that the two year Caesarean imprisonment is a valid datum, and that the two year imprisonment in Rome is likewise valid. The departure from Philippi offers dates in two of the twelve years, producing a probability of 1:6; that the Festus accession to office falls on a coordinated year has a probability of 1:12; that Ananias is in office at the time of Paul's arrival was true for seven of the twelve years in question, producing a probability of 7:12; the probable *terminus a quo* for the Egyptian rebel is more than eight years from the end of the base period, so the odds are 8:12; the arrival in Rome should be prior to the end of A.D. 61, so the chances here of a correlation are 9:12; the departure from Fair Havens works best in one year out of 12, producing odds of 1:12; and Paul's execution occurred in a period between the spring of A.D. 62 and the summer of 64, approximately 30 months out of a potential of 144 months, producing odds of 30:144. The formula $E_1$ times $E_2$ times $E_3$ times $E_4$ times $E_5$ times $E_6$ times $E_7$ produces odds of 1:14,169.6 for all seven dates and time–spans coordinating within a twelve year period.

26. An example of the potentially fruitful interplay between chronology

and the development of early Christianity is provided by Martin Hengel, "Christologie und neutestamentliche Chronologie: Zu einer Aporie in der Geschichte des Urchristentums," *Neues Testament und Geschichte: Oscar Cullmann zum 70. Geburtstag,* ed. H. Baltensweiler & B. Reicke (Tübingen: Mohr–Siebeck, 1972), 43–67.

# INDEX OF AUTHORS

# INDEX OF PASSAGES

## NEW TESTAMENT

## OLD TESTAMENT

## GREEK AND ROMAN LITERATURE

# GRAPH OF DATES AND TIME-SPANS

# GRAPH OF DATES AND TIME-SPANS

| AD: | EXTERNALLY ASCERTAINABLE DATE-RANGES | INTERNALLY ASCERTAINABLE DATES AND TIME-SPANS | RESULTANT PAULINE CHRONOLOGY |
|---|---|---|---|
| 30 | April 7—less probable date of crucifixion<br><br>Traditional eighteen month span of resurrection appearances | (The length of these time-spans is well established but their placement on the graph results from correlations with other data, and reflects the results of the experimental hypothesis.) | (Estimated *termini a quo et ad quem* for writing the authentic Pauline letters are assigned at locations that appear most plausible for future investigations. All other dates and time-spans are discussed or directly implied in the relevant portions of the study.) |
| 31 | October 7 or 12 | | |
| 32 | | | |
| 33 | April 3—more probable date of crucifixion<br><br>Traditional eighteen month span of resurrection appearances | | |
| 34 | October 3 or 8 | | October Conversion |
| 35 | | Possible three year span between conversion and first Jerusalem journey | Activities |
| 36 | | | in Arabia & return to |
| 37 | | | Damascus |

Escape from Aretas IV & 1st Jerusalem journey

Expedition from Antioch to Cyprus, Pamphylia, and South Galatia (= 1st missionary journey)

Activities in Syria and Cilicia

March sailing Antioch to Salamis

**Possible full fourteen year span between first Jerusalem Journey and Apostolic Conference**

Aretas IV begins to control Damascus

Paul evades the ethnarch of Aretas IV

Death of Aretas IV

| 38 | 39 | 40 | 41 | 42 | 43 | 44 | 45 |

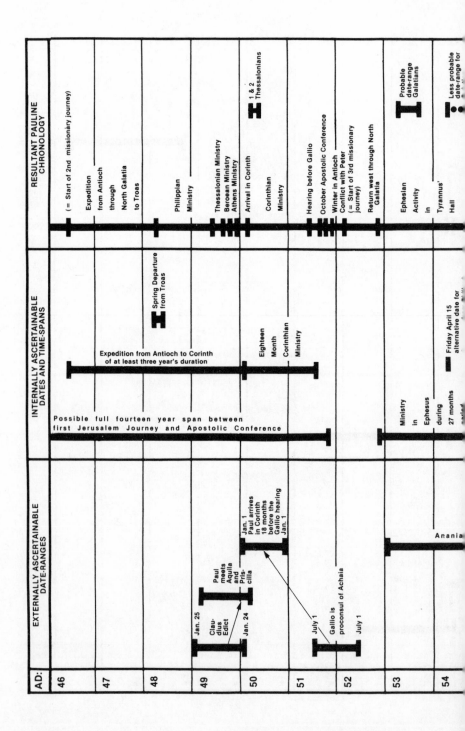

| AD: | EXTERNALLY ASCERTAINABLE DATE-RANGES | INTERNALLY ASCERTAINABLE DATES AND TIME-SPANS | RESULTANT PAULINE CHRONOLOGY |
|---|---|---|---|
| 46 | | | (= Start of 2nd missionary journey) |
| 47 | | | Expedition from Antioch through North Galatia to Troas |
| 48 | | Spring Departure from Troas | Philippian Ministry |
| 49 | Jan. 25 Claudius Edict — Jan. 24 / Paul meets Aquila and Priscilla | Expedition from Antioch to Corinth of at least three year's duration | Thessalonian Ministry / Beroean Ministry / Athens Ministry |
| 50 | Jan. 1 Paul arrives in Corinth 18 months before the Gallio hearing / Jan. 1 | Eighteen Month Corinthian Ministry | Arrival in Corinth / 1 & 2 Thessalonians / Corinthian Ministry |
| 51 | July 1 Gallio is proconsul of Achaia July 1 | | Hearing before Gallio / October Apostolic Conference |
| 52 | | | Winter in Antioch / Conflict with Peter (= Start of 3rd missionary journey) / Return west through North Galatia |
| 53 | Anania | Ministry In Ephesus during 27 months ... | Ephesian Activity In Tyrannus' Hall / Probable date-range Galatians |
| 54 | | Friday April 15 alternative date for ... | Less probable date-range for ... |

Possible full fourteen year span between first Jerusalem Journey and Apostolic Conference

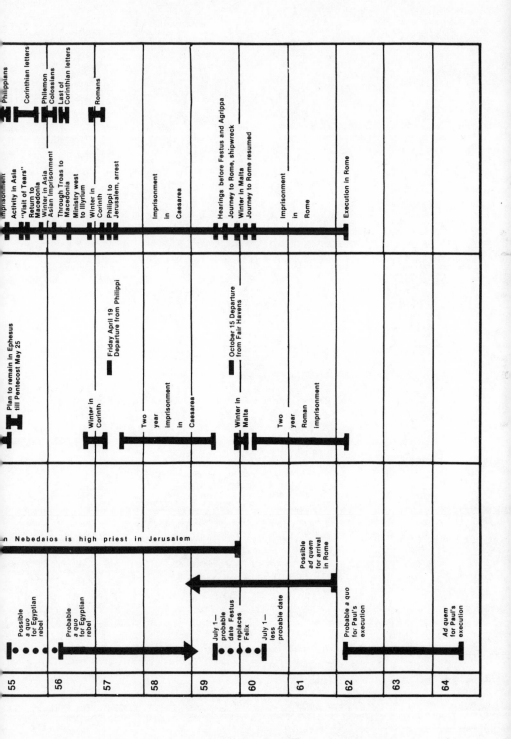